D1569340

"Financial Freedom is the confidence that comes from putting money in its place!"

—Jenifer Madson

A FINANCIAL
m:nute

Here's what people are saying about Jenifer's work:

Keeping *A Financial Minute* handy for weekly reference is a splendid way to have a "portable financial coach" close at hand.
    —*Cecile Schoberle, Denver, CO, Creative Direction/Brand Strategies*

After I saw Jenifer Madson speak, I booked her on my radio show as a weekly guest. She gives you the information you need in a language you can understand.
    —*Jo Myers, Denver, CO, KOSI-FM Morning Show Host*

Jenifer has an extraordinary gift for helping people shed their money hang-ups so they can enjoy greater personal freedom, financial prosperity and professional success in their lives.
    —*Margie Warrell, McLean, VA, Life Coach*

Jenifer has the uncanny ability to see through our actions to unearth our motives. With her help, nothing is impossible.
    —*James Dibella, New York, NY, Commodities Broker*

Jenifer's compassion, wisdom, and boldness were what I needed to move forward financially. I only wish I'd met her sooner!
    —*Mandy Pratt, Boise, ID, Real Estate Agent, Life Coach*

The information in *A Financial Minute* is something that those of us in need of a financial "attitude adjustment" really need to hear. This has truly given me hope for the future!
    —*Regina Dunay, Orlando, FL, Career Consultant*

A Financial Minute is truly a gift to anyone who is striving to reach his or her fullest potential!
    —*Heather Graham, Glen Burnie, MD, School Counselor*

Jenifer helped make my financial dreams a reality. Anyone who has the experience of working with her has found someone very special.
    —*Anna Macgowan, Melbourne, Australia, Life Coach*

The wisdom and organization of Jenifer's step-by-step process in *A Financial Minute* has helped me create more success in three weeks with her program than all of last year!

—*Lissa Forbes, Lafayette, CO, Niche Publisher, Author*

Jenifer asks all the right questions. She is part philosopher, part cheerleader and has some really healthy attitudes towards money. If there is such a thing as a good virus, she may be contagious.

—*Teri Tith, Toronto, Ontario, Creative Director*

Anyone can teach you a budget, but *A Financial Minute* helps you dig deeper through all the old beliefs and come up with a vision and a plan that motivates you to make money work for you.

—*Jaye Bell, Aurora, CO, Mortgage Loan Processor*

A good coach helps you figure out how to reach your defined goals. A *GREAT* coach helps you determine what steps will serve your highest good and manifest your true heart's desire. Jenifer has the energy and commitment of a *GREAT* coach, no matter what is happening in your life.

—*Marilyn Kier, Chicago, IL, Massage Therapist*

Through my work with Jenifer, I've learned to focus on money-making activities that are fulfilling in ways well beyond the balance in my checking account. Money now flows through my life more easily.

—*Clare Kelly, Denver, CO, Real Estate Investor*

Most families have an elephant under the carpet in their living room named Money. *A Financial Minute* helps you take one chunk of the elephant out at a time, so you don't trip on Money anymore.

—*Jade Sund, Broomfield, CO, Personal Coach*

I love that the main focus in *A Financial Minute* is how to change one's thinking about money versus changing how much money I can "make" come to me.

—*Marlena McElhaney, Aurora, CO, Stay-at-home Mom*

Jenifer taught me how to pinpoint what steps my husband and I needed to take in order to save for our future. I sleep better now knowing we made these decisions with confidence and were well informed of our choices.

—*Joanne Dee, Baltimore, MD, Professional Bookbinder*

Jenifer exemplifies her message of abundance. Her passion for life is contagious, her energy boundless, her *Financial Minute*, priceless.

—*Pamela McCreary, Highlands Ranch, CO, Author, Magazine Editor*

Jenifer's work was key in producing an important transformation in my life: I found the courage to not be afraid—to put faith in front of fear as she puts it—and to trust that I can do what I love and make a living at it.

—*Maggie Macnab, Albuquerque, NM, Symbolist/Graphic Designer*

Jenifer helped me and my husband manifest our dream of bringing in an abundant income from doing what we love. When it comes to finance, Jenifer is a strategic spiritual advisor!

—*Cathie Soderman, Nederland, CO, President, Warrior Artists Films*

I use Jen's *Financial Minutes* as a roadmap, which tells me whether I am on course or veering off towards a ravine! She offers an impressive combination of practical, strategic, and spiritual advice regarding money.

—*Regina Weichert, Martha's Vineyard, MA, Performance Artist*

Read and re-read *A Financial Minute*. Jenifer's insight into the power of managing your thoughts about money will put you back in control of creating your own financial abundance. And remember, the more you have, the more you can give.

—*Will Matthews, Westminster, CO, Executive Coach*

Jenifer has helped me shape my life into a happier, more purposeful one.   —*Laura Stein, Orlando, FL, Office Manager*

Jenifer has an incredible ability to make the sometimes complex subject of finances easy to understand. Her advice in *A Financial Minute* is simple, straight-forward, and easy to apply.

—*Kimberly Fulcher, San Jose, CA, Author—Remodel Your Reality*

Instead of trying to impress the reader with how smart she is, Jen motivates each reader internally by providing them with open, flexible, honest insights for how money might work for them. No pretense, no shame—just good stuff you can actually use.

—*Brandy Bertram, Denver, CO, Deputy Director, Non-profit*

Something Jenifer said has propelled me to more financial success than I've ever had: *"Many people think they will be happy when they have money. In fact, when you are happy, you will attract money."*

—*Denise Arand, Littleton, CO, Investment Professional*

Jenifer's ability to engage the crowd during her presentations on money issues is remarkable. There is never a dull moment when Jenifer speaks...we listen, we absorb, and we get it!

—*Julie Johnson, Portland, OR, Marketing Director, Financial Services*

Jenifer helps "create the means" to have a healthy relationship with family, work, and money. Now I'm addicted to saving my time and money, and I love my business again.

—*Kelly Grady, Aurora, CO, Wholesale Diamond and Jewelry Broker*

Because of Jenifer's programs, I feel as if I'm finally in control of my money and on a path that is getting me to the life I have always wanted. I am truly grateful she and I crossed paths.

—*Meghan Starmer, Denver, CO, Mortgage Account Manager*

I truly appreciate how Jenifer helps to extract and enhance what is working within my monetary belief system, and to toss out what isn't. The tools I have gained are continuously useful, as well as creative and FUN! —*Lisa Fierer, Boulder, CO, Small Business Owner*

Jenifer has offered me one of the most valuable gifts of my lifetime—the support I needed to believe in my own vision and bring it forth into the world.

—*Megan Walrod, Boulder, CO, Transition Consultant*

Jen doesn't talk about how to make a million dollars overnight—she shares insights into how anyone can better manage their finances to achieve their own dreams. And best of all, she practices what she preaches!

—*Lara K. Loest, Denver, CO, Small Business Development*

Jen's commitment to helping people comes through as clearly in her actions as it does in her writing. Her support for low-income urban youth to improve their economic knowledge has a benefit that cannot be measured but should truly be treasured—just like *A Financial Minute* should.

—*Edwin Velis, Denver, CO, Micro Enterprise Development*

Jenifer is very skilled at helping one get down to business about starting and running a business, using practical guidance along with compassionate understanding as I work to bring my vision to reality.

—*Chris Trani, Arvada, CO, Consultant*

Jenifer's program helped break me out of a downward spiral financially and emotionally. She accepted who I was, didn't blink an eye at any of my self-perceived "financial sins," and worked with me to help me get closer to my goals.

—*Laura Maynor, Denver, CO, Marketing Communications Manager*

Jenifer is particularly artful in helping people identify their values and then regularly matching their money to those.

—*Pam Dumonceau, Denver, CO, Registered Investment Advisor*

CLEAR VISION PRESS

D E N V E R

Clear Vision Press
2382 Norfolk St., Erie, CO 80516
(303) 664-1947 main, (303) 484-4937 fax
info@afinancialminute.com

www.afinancialminute.com

PRINTED IN THE UNITED STATES OF AMERICA

Publisher's Cataloging-In-Publication
    Madson, Jenifer
        A Financial Minute: From money madness to financial freedom, one minute
        at a time/
    Jenifer Madson.—1st ed.—Erie, CO : Clear Vision Press, 2006 p. ; cm
        "Finally, common sense and money collide."
    Includes bibliographical information, appendix and index.
    ISBN: 0-9777770-2-2
        1. Women—Personal Finance   2. Self-help—Personal Finance
        3. Women—Life Skills guides   4. Wealth—Psychological aspects   I. Title
    332.0240082—dc22

Cover design, illustration and interior layout: Melanie Warner, Hotiron Creative Group
Indexing: Christine Frank
Editor: Cindy Troast

A FINANCIAL
m:nute

Jenifer Madson

*To my amazing husband Les, who taught me
"the good news," and always sees more
possibility than anyone I know.
Thank you for the kisses, cookies and critiques—
they always came at just the right time!*

ACKNOWLEDGMENTS 1

A WORD FROM THE AUTHOR 5

INTRODUCTION: The Romance Of Finance 9

PART *one:* WHAT DO YOU *think?*

:01 Once Upon A Time... 17

:02 Have Faith 23

:03 Ommmmm 29

:04 Blue Light Special! 33

:05 You're Enough Without Your Stuff 37

:06 Practice Makes Perfect 43

:07 Great Expectations 49

:08 Back To The Future! 53

PART *two:* WHAT DO YOU *say?*

:09 Watch Your Language 59

:10 The $64,000 Question 65

:11 Wants Vs. Needs 71

:12 What's In A Word? 77

:13 Neither A Borrower Nor A
     Lender Be...Right? 81

:14   Dollars & Sense   85

:15   Mind Your Manners   89

:16   The Energy Of Money   93

PART *three:* WHAT DO YOU *do?*

:17   Budget Your Balance   99

:18   Call In The Troops   105

:19   How Do You Spell Relief?   109

:20   Step Away From The Remote!   113

:21   Acting "As If"   117

:22   K.I.S.S. (Keep It Simple, Sweetie!)   123

:23   Chuck, Merrill Or Raymond?   127

:24   You, CEO   131

CONCLUSION: Rolling Around Naked
In A Pile Of Money   137

APPENDIX A: Budget Form   143

APPENDIX B: Save...And Walk Tall   145

RESOURCES   147

INDEX   151

BIO & CONTACT INFORMATION   156

Acknowledgments

Everyone knows that it takes a lot of people to create a book, and I've been looking forward to acknowledging the people who contributed to this project since it began. My thanks go to:

Debbie Phillips, my coach, who has been such an amazing life preserver while I tested the waters of authorship and publishing. She is the warmest person I know, and I am blessed to be in her circle.

To her partner, Rob Berkley, who brought his considerable talents as an executive coach to bear on my marketing efforts, in particular, the formatting of my weekly e-column, "A Financial Minute w/Jenifer," from which this book was sprung.

To my first coach Becca Robinson—for helping me know what coaching is, supporting me in my decision to be one, and for being a great friend.

To my brothers and sisters, in-laws and outlaws—Tom and Deb, John, Katie, Christopher and Ruth and J.B.—who always find time to give me encouragement, no matter how many miles separate us.

To the Madsons, who have treated me from day one as one of their own and also offered their encouragement and support.

To Jan King of eWomenPublishingNetwork who gave such clear,

unbiased advice as I put this book together, thank you for your encouragement, knowledge, and support

To Cindy Troast, my editor—you made me a better writer and helped me keep my wits about me!

To contributing editors Margaret Sewall and Joyanna Laughlin, thank you for your talents and your feedback.

To my Dad, Don Glancy and my stepmother Janet, for so willingly stepping in with your considerable literary talents to finalize the manuscript and see that it got delivered on time. Thank you both for your unquestioning support.

To the literary agents who graciously gave me the feedback I needed to make this happen.

To Melanie Warner and Jeff Norgord, the design team for the book—for your great creative minds. My book wouldn't have the energy it has without you. Thanks for being so wonderfully patient with me.

To the people along the way who, without even knowing me, were willing to share their excitement about the book. In particular, I want to thank Linda Sivertsen for her contribution to my original proposal.

To Mandy Pratt, Cindy Troast, Alison Fleming, Will Matthews, and Diane Sieg, my major, good coaching buddies, who did such an awesome job of indulging my insanity and provided such expert, on-the-spot mentoring for me.

To Ann Vertel, with whom I created a mastermind alliance that knows no bounds. You're my hero in so many ways!

To the Managing Directors of eWomenNetwork who threw their doors open to promote this, particularly Melissa Haines Shults, Marsha Livingston, Mary Pearsall and Susan Wight.

To my book club buddies, Jaye Bell, Heather Graham, and Candy Donaldson. Thank you for listening patiently as I talked over and over about when this would finally be done, and for "keeping it real!"

To Brandy Bertram and the staff at Micro Business Development in Denver, for partnering with me on so many levels in the last several years to bring my message to those they serve. I appreciate our partnership more than you know.

To Jo Myers, Murphy Houston and Gov Landrum, at KOSI-FM radio in Denver, for taking a chance on me and being good friends.

To fellow coaches the world over, for doing what you do to help people live more fulfilling lives.

To my clients, past, present, and future, for your willingness to open up, share your struggles, have faith and make changes.

To my friends, for your general fabulousness!

To my mom, Karen Glancy, who since I was young has seen a bigger vision for me than I could sometimes see for myself. Thank you for always supporting me, even when tough love was the best way to do it.

To Missy and Jazz, my "girls," for making me play when I didn't think I had time, and keeping me company in the middle of the night when the work had to be done. They can't read this, but I'll read it to them and they'll kiss me all over again.

And again, to Les, for always believing in all that was possible for me and for us. I love you more than I can say.

A Word From The Author

Most people assume I've always been good with money, since I hold myself out as an expert on the subject. A part of me wishes that were true.

The bigger part of me is grateful for my financial mistakes because they let me relate to you from a place of deeper understanding. Without them, this book would be two-thirds speculation, one-third experience. As it is, the depth of my past financial drama brings a certain wisdom to the subject, and from that I want you to know two things by the time we're done: that you don't have to hit rock bottom like I did before you can change, and financial success isn't as hard as you think.

Here's the short version of what I've been through:

I never learned anything about money growing up. I had jobs, but I never had any money that I remember. My financial pattern was simple: I spent more than I earned and relied on the kindness of friends, family, and strangers to bail me out. The situations were embarrassing but not dramatic enough to make me change my behavior.

I figured that sooner or later my money troubles would work

themselves out. Seriously, I thought someone would eventually have a money talk with me much the same way you educate kids on the birds and the bees. Then I would have the information I needed to be financially responsible. I was wrong. There was no such meeting coming. Like almost everyone I've met, I had to learn money lessons the hard way.

And financial opportunity kept knocking, even though I wasn't equipped to handle it. I worked a variety of jobs in my twenties, and always made good money, but I never learned to do anything more with it than spend more than I made. I was bright, but uninformed and unmotivated, so I was still broke most of the time.

I bought a dating service franchise in my early thirties and started making a significant amount of money. I had great intentions of using that income to turn my financial life around. But my pride kept me from learning what the financial professionals tried to teach me. I was too embarrassed to admit what I didn't know about money, so I convinced myself that I was "too right-brained" to learn it anyway, and subconsciously distanced myself from the very information I needed to survive professionally.

After a few years, my dating business took a turn for the worse, and since I couldn't learn the financial strategies I needed in time to reverse the downward spiral, I lost it all: the business, my house, my savings, and a lot of material stuff.

It was a devastating and intensely shameful experience. I didn't know how I would recover, much less whether I could. All I could think about was how defeated I felt. But a funny thing happened on the way to putting my life back together: I kept meeting people who were determined to see more for me than I could for myself. And deep inside I really wanted to believe life could be better, so I held on to their dreams until I could find my own.

My financial recovery started when I was offered an opportunity to work in mortgage lending and financial services. I accepted the invitation—not because it seemed logical, but because I had to have something to move on to. I was very uncomfortable in those industries at first, because I didn't know how I could help others when I hadn't been able to help myself. Back then I didn't even know how to use a calculator beyond the basics. Fortunately, I found mentors who agreed to teach me financial concepts as long as I committed to applying them personally. They taught me how to bring financial security back into my life—how to calculate investment returns, qualify for a mortgage and get money back in the bank. And as I changed my ways with money, I found the confidence to teach others how to do the same.

In the beginning of that career, I assumed that all one needed for financial success was to know the technical aspects of how money works. I soon realized that people's beliefs about money had an even greater influence on their results.

I began to spend more time working with people on those belief systems and saw hundreds of them reach their goals as a result of shifting their attitudes about money, myself included. Those experiences are what led me to leave the licensed side of the money business and become a coach. When I was in the midst of fiscal ruin, I couldn't have known to what degree that experience would lead me to aid others in finding financial peace, but I am grateful that it has. In addition, I have each of my clients to thank for having the courage to share their struggles. They have taught me a great deal and have generously let me pass that knowledge on so that others can also grow.

．
．

So, what does this mean for you? It means that I will share what I know about how to think, speak, and act your way to financial success. We'll start in your head, with what you think about money, and give you the tools to see success as your destiny. Then we'll move on to new language skills, including how to enroll others in your success. Finally, we'll talk about action steps to support your goals, from budgeting to picking the right financial professionals.

I have synchronized stories, tools, and exercises that will transform your financial experience. Based on where you are with money, some of the lessons will be easy, some may be a stretch. All of them are designed to improve your circumstances in some way. So grab a journal, or use the space provided, and make time to work these steps into your life. When we're done, I promise you'll never feel the same about money again.

∙
∙

Someone once asked me, "How did you come from all that financial pain to where you are today?" My answer: "One minute at a time, one choice at a time, one day at a time." Make the next twenty-four *Minutes* your own, and your life will be simpler and more fulfilled than you can imagine!

The Romance Of Finance

Money is a mystery, just like love, and the questions for success are pretty much the same: how do you attract it, keep it, and make it grow?

Establishing a positive relationship with money is no different from finding success in our other associations. It takes communication, which leads to a close connection with the subject, and that familiarity or intimacy is what leads to success. So in order to achieve the level of intimacy with money that we demand in our other relationships, we must start talking about it and be determined to get the information we need to succeed.

Our dilemma is that money is such a taboo topic that it's not even included with sex, politics, and religion in the list of top things not to discuss. Throw in some negative associations—that money is the enemy or that it holds some superhuman power—and you have all the reasons you need to stay quiet about it. And if you can't talk about it, how are you supposed to know what to do with it?

Mostly, we keep money matters to ourselves because we learned so little about it growing up that we don't know what to say about it now. It's certainly easier to say nothing than to let someone see your ignorance, but that only perpetuates the cycle of misinformation and doubt. It takes a lot of courage to break this pattern, but it can be done, if your motivation is strong.

This book teaches you how to talk about money so you can find peace with it, starting with empowering things to say to yourself about it. Strong internal beliefs open the door to constructive conversation with others, which is the key to getting the financial details you need to succeed.

Laurie:

Laurie was a client from the dating service I owned. She loved to talk about her desires in a mate and saw me as her ally in an exciting new adventure. She met suggestions, like a change in hairstyle or wardrobe, with remarkable commitment. She wasn't the least bit shy when it came to discussing her romantic interests and was confident that being introspective and purposeful would bring her happiness.

Then we started talking about money; and she resisted.

When it came to discussing the impact of money on her relationships, she wouldn't hear of it. Her marriage had ended, as so many do, over financial issues, so she stubbornly insisted on keeping the subject out of her future relationships.

"True love conquers all," she said, and she meant it. You know how the story ends: those who forget the past are doomed to repeat it, and by ignoring signs of financial incompatibility, she continued to waste time dating men who weren't right for her.

One day, when she came in to update her profile, she said, "I give in. Find me someone who can balance his checkbook."

"Don't you want someone who has better financial qualities than that?" I asked.

"Baby steps, Jenifer, baby steps," Laurie told me.

Laurie had discovered her mistake in blaming money for the problems in her marriage. The truth was they'd had plenty of money; they just hadn't shared the same values about it. They hadn't discovered this until it was too late because they had rarely discussed it, and when they did, it was always a fight.

So the first step she took with her dates was to talk about money from a standpoint of general curiosity, just to expand her capacity for conversation about it and learn more about her own financial values.

She learned a lot about what mattered to her financially, and used that information to make more definitive choices about whom she would date. Her dating experiences changed dramatically because she honored these new standards, which eventually led her to an exclusive relationship with someone she felt compatible with on all levels.

Six months later, thinking back on her initial resistance to the subject of money and love, she looked me straight in the eye and said, "I always wanted to be financially compatible. I just didn't want to have to talk about it!"

Take A Minute:

The first conversation to have in your quest for financial freedom is with yourself, to see if you're ready to open up about money and let others accompany you on that journey.

Start by answering the following questions:

- What are your current financial circumstances?

_____

_____

_____

_____

_____

_____

- Where do you want to be financially?

_____

_____

_____

_____

_____

_____

- What are you willing to change about yourself to get what you want?

_____

_____

_____

_____

_____

_____

- Whom will you ask for help in making these changes?

_____

_____

_____

_____

_____

_____

If you're strongly committed to change, you've made a great start. Determination is the best foundation on which to build a vision of the future.

Make A Minute:

The next step to lasting financial change is to get your concerns out of your head and into the open.

- Commit to telling one person today about the financial shifts you want to make.

Make Another Minute:

Record what was different or better for you from having that conversation.

_____

_____

_____

_____

_____

_____

.
.

These are the first steps to becoming intimately familiar with how money works. As you can see, it doesn't have to be that difficult. Take the right steps, develop them into habits, and you'll have a relationship with money that can sustain you for life!

PART one

WHAT DO YOU *think?*

CHAPTER one

Once Upon A Time...

:01 If you had to pick a fairy tale that described your experience with money, which one would it be? I hope you're not Cinderella, waiting for your Fairy Godmother to transport you to a better financial place, or Sleeping Beauty, oblivious to what's happening with the money around you. Maybe you're Prince Charming himself, looking for your damsel in financial distress. None of these sound like the role of a lifetime, do they!

Your "money story," or what you believe is financially possible, has a bigger influence on your success than education, social advantage, or the right job. So, when it comes to financial success, you're in charge of your happy ending. And since I couldn't find a fairy tale to borrow that didn't rely on a heroic rescue for its happily-ever-after, we'll just have to write one in which you free yourself.

If there's a negative story in your head about money, chances are you're living with unfavorable financial circumstances to match. The good news is you can reverse the trend. You can simply choose a better belief about money, then create an environment to support it. Your beliefs will drive your actions, and through your actions you'll manifest results. Imagine an entirely new and exciting financial ending, simply by beginning from stronger beliefs.

Lisa:

Lisa came to me because her financial life was one fire drill after another. Nothing was getting paid on time, and many bills weren't getting paid at all. When we examined what was going on, we discovered that she made more than enough money to meet her expenses. So, what was the problem?

Lisa had grown up in a house where money was always a struggle. Her parents fought constantly about how to make ends meet. She distinctly remembers the Formica and metal kitchen table at her parents' house, the bills spread all over the top, where these discussions would take place. She recalls her mother saying repeatedly, "We're in such a mess." And indeed, they were.

As an adult, Lisa found herself falling into similar habits. Making money was never the issue—she made a decent living. She wasn't that foolish about spending either. The problem was Lisa had learned that money equaled "messy," and unconsciously behaved in a way that reflected that belief. She routinely let bills pile up, which is why they didn't get paid on time. When she got behind paying bills, she incurred late fees and overdraft charges because she wasn't balancing her checkbook either.

What made Lisa's behavior all the more confusing was that it was the complete opposite of her professional performance. At work she was neat, organized, and on time with tasks. Why be on the ball for your boss and not at home?

Our conversations revealed that she was afraid to pull ahead financially because of how she thought it would affect her relationship with her parents. They had never found their way to financial peace, and she didn't want them to feel bad as a result of her success.

:

Take A Minute:

Ask yourself these questions about your current money story:

- What beliefs am I holding that don't support me?

_____

_____

_____

_____

- What environment have I created to mirror those beliefs?

_____

_____

_____

_____

- What actions do I take accordingly?

_____

_____

_____

_____

- What are my results?

_____

_____

_____

_____

- What is my payoff from continuing to hold those beliefs?

_____

_____

_____

_____

"Payoff" is the idea that even if we're getting a negative result in our lives, we stay there because we're getting something out of it in spite of the pain. The payoff may be the attention that comes from our drama or the slack someone cuts us out of sympathy for our situation. There's always a payoff for staying where we are, and it's important to identify it and choose whether it's supportive to hang on to it.

Make A Minute:

Now let's choose what you want to believe about money:
- Write a new belief about money in the present tense. For example, instead of writing "Money can...." write "Money is...."

_____

_____

_____

_____

- Commit to three actions that immediately create an environment consistent with that belief.

_____

_____

_____

- Commit to three daily actions to support that environment.

_____

_____

_____

•
•
•

What are the results you'll get by writing a new story?

While going through this exercise, Lisa wrote, "Money supports what I love," choosing to see it as something of value, rather than as a source of pain. She then aligned her surroundings with that belief. She got very organized and created a system for where the bills would land when they came in, how they would get paid, and where they would get filed when she had paid them. The payoff from her old behavior was in not having to find a new way to relate to her parents; as long as they had the financial mess in common, they had something to talk about. Becoming more efficient in how she handled her money freed up time to develop a more meaningful relationship with them, which was a much bigger payoff in the end.

Her newfound enthusiasm for financial organization also motivated her parents to become more organized, and after a while, Lisa saw the top of their kitchen table for the first time in many years.

．
．
．

You don't have to live by old stories that don't work for you today. The beliefs you've just created are the first of many new chapters. They've put the wheels in motion for a new future with money, and by continuing to strengthen the environment that supports them, you will have more peace of mind than you ever thought possible.

CHAPTER *two*

Have Faith

:02 You've made a commitment to change your financial habits and have started to create new belief systems. That doesn't mean your financial fears have vanished. You might still feel some doubts about how to put money to work for you and whether you're up to the challenge.

I've heard the only thing bigger than fear is faith, but if you're in a difficult spot with money, it can be a challenge to find faith, much less put it to good use. Since there probably isn't a more effective tool than faith in the fight for financial freedom, we'll learn to give it the attention *and* intention it needs to support that part of your life.

You & Me:

What is faith? The automatic answer might be the belief in God or some other deity. Some people might characterize it as confidence. One Merriam-Webster dictionary definition is: "needs firm belief in something for which there is no proof."

For me, faith is an unexplainable certainty that forces bigger than me are at work in my life. The paradox of faith is that strength comes from surrender—when I turn things over to a force greater than myself I gain more power than I could ever manufacture on my own.

Take A Minute:
- What does faith mean to you?

_____

_____

_____

_____

⋮

You & Me, Continued:

Where does faith come from? We won't get into a chicken-and-egg discussion about which comes first, faith or results, although one great book does suggest that faith precedes the miracle. There are times when I've got faith first and results follow, and sometimes it's the other way around. I'm always better off when I invite faith to run the show. I am much calmer when I foster faith before I act, than the reverse.

Prayer and meditation are my physical acts of faith. And when I put aside projections of the future and remind myself to stay in the present, I consider that a mental act of faith.

Overall, I believe or have faith that the present is perfect in some way, and I consistently remind myself to honor the evidence of that.

Take Another Minute:
- How do you engage your faith?

_____

_____

_____

_____

·
·
·

So why does faith matter when it comes to our money?

Because it beats the alternative, which is to allow fear to overtake us and keep us from taking the actions we need to succeed financially. I know few people who live a life completely free of fear. I think the best we can do when it shows up is to examine what's driving it, and agree to have at least an equal amount of faith.

·
·
·

It's been said that FEAR is an acronym for **F**alse **E**vidence **A**ppearing **R**eal. When it comes to overcoming your financial fears, the first step is to separate which ones are real and which are imagined. Then you can choose a reaction appropriate to the circumstances, and save yourself unnecessary anxiety in the process.

Make A Minute:

- Write three of your financial fears and ask yourself whether they're real or made up. If they are real (if you have solid evidence to support them), find something you can have faith in—no matter what—that can help the situation. Then commit to actions to back up that faith.

Example:

You tell yourself:

I'm afraid I won't have enough money to retire.

You decide that it's real, based on this evidence:

I'm 55, have no savings, and have large debts.

The next question you would ask is:

What can I have faith in, that can help this situation?

Your answers might be:

I have faith that I can learn new skills to improve my income. I have faith I can learn to reverse my debt. I have faith I can do something to change today.

The actions might be:

I will learn the new computer program I need for a promotion. I will outline a payback system for my debt.

If you can't find evidence to support your fears, re-write them starting with "It's not true that..." and finish with "...because..."

Example:

It's not true that I won't have enough money to retire because I will learn how much money it takes and adjust my budget to accommodate it.

Fear #1: _____

Evidence?

_____

_____

Faith?

_____

_____

Actions?

_____

_____

Rewrite?

_____

_____

Fear #2: _____

Evidence?

_____

_____

Faith?

_____

_____

Actions?

_____

_____

Rewrite?

_____

_____

Fear #3: _____

Evidence?

_____

_____

Faith?

_____

_____

Actions?

_____

_____

Rewrite?

_____

_____

Make Another Minute:

- Write five affirmations of financial faith—five things that you are absolutely certain of, no matter what the circumstances.

Examples:

I have faith I can learn how money works.
I have faith in my ability to grow.
I have faith in the support of great friends and family.

1.

_____

_____

2.

_____

_____

3.

_____

_____

4.

_____

_____

5.

_____

_____

⋮

Always find more to believe in than to fear, and don't be afraid to ask for help in this process. I've had a lot of people that believed in me until I could believe in myself. I had to borrow their faith for a long time, until I could build some of my own. If you still don't have the personal faith you need, figure out whose you can borrow—I'm sure they'll have some to spare. If you already have tons of internal guidance, look for ways to share that with others until they find their way.

CHAPTER three

Ommmmm

:03 Chanting. Meditation. Prayer. All over the world, people lift their voices and thoughts to the heavens to raise their consciousness, improve their circumstances, and to be of better service. We just talked about faith—the knowledge that we're meant for more than our struggles indicate. But faith alone is not enough to get us to our goals. We must put that faith into action by directing our focus accordingly.

When it comes to money, where is your focus? Does your mind go to what you have, or veer to what's missing? More than a half-empty or half-full mentality, do you focus on the mistakes of the past, or the possibilities of the future? Are you directing your focus, or allowing it to direct you?

My Story:

Here's what I know about focus: As I related earlier, growing up I knew nothing about how money worked. From the time I got my first job at Kentucky Fried Chicken™ until I was into my late twenties, I was focused on just getting by. I didn't have a vision of prosperity; I was living paycheck to paycheck. With that focus of "just enough," what do you think I got? You've got it: just enough. The funny thing was, as my income kept going up I stayed in "just enough" because I didn't change my focus to match my circumstances.

When I was finally in a business that brought me a significant amount of money, my focus was more on how to spend it than how to keep it. How do you think that ended? Badly. When the tides of that business changed, and I needed to focus my attention on how to keep it going, I didn't know how to adjust and I lost the whole thing.

As I emerged from that business failure, I chose to take a good, hard look at what I wanted for my life and what part I wanted money to play in it. In the beginning, all I could focus on was, "I'm meant for more than this," "this" being the pain of scarcity and loss. It was difficult to hold that focus early on because my experiences pointed to something pretty different.

With the help of a lot of people and prayer, I stopped listening to the committee in my head that said I was doomed to fail. Instead, I started paying attention to the still, small voice inside that told me there was something positive ahead, that I just needed to prepare my mind for it. Eventually, I was able to focus on what I now believe I'm specifically meant for, which is to better myself for the sake of those I can help.

I spend some part of every day reinforcing that focus, sometimes in my head, thinking about what I want, sometimes on paper, actually mapping it out. The result is that money comes and money goes. Some stays to support my future and some leaves to support others. Rather than focusing on what I need, I focus on how I can serve. My peace of mind comes from knowing that, for me, this is how it's meant to be.

Take A Minute:

- What are you focused on financially?

_____

_____

_____

- What are the results?

_____

_____

_____

- Do you direct your focus or does it direct you?

_____

_____

_____

Make A Minute:

I asked you earlier to examine your beliefs about money in a general way. Now we'll develop a more specific, guiding Money Mantra: a personal statement of purpose, intention, or belief that drives your new financial identity.

- Sit comfortably. Imagine what you'd like to be true about you and your money. What do you look like when you're in that place? What feelings come with being there? Let a smile visit your face as though you've arrived. (And if you have, smile even bigger!) Really let yourself be in that vision—that place of whatever success looks like to you.
- Now, take your thoughts and feelings and boil them down to a statement about you and your money that brings that same energy and calm, sweet smile to your being. This will be your Money Mantra.

_____

_____

_____

_____

_____

_____

Here's mine:

I am open to accept what is mine to receive, and happy to let go of what will find better service elsewhere.

Focusing daily on my mantra brings me incredible peace on my financial journey.

Make Another Minute:

The second step, as I just mentioned, is to engage that focus every day.

- Write your Money Mantra on something you can easily carry with you.
- Schedule your focus time—and commit to meditating on that mantra, even if only for a few minutes.
- Record what changes result from this practice.

_____

_____

_____

_____

_____

_____

⋮

If you want to achieve your goals, you need to visualize them *and* direct your energy to specific actions for realizing them. You have to engage your faith—through the act of focus—to get results. That means doing everything you can to focus first on what really serves you and others, and then taking the steps to manifest it.

CHAPTER four

Blue Light Special!

:04 "Blue light special!" was a call to action that blared over the speakers of certain discount stores, announcing the phenomenal bargains awaiting us on aisle five. It didn't matter what we already had in our baskets, that siren said that something better was yet to be had. All we had to do was get there. Our marketing culture still uses the allure of more, better, faster to entice us, making it easy to get caught up in the promise of tomorrow, to the neglect of today.

Kim:

Kim was a prime example of someone so focused on the future and how things "should" be that she had lost touch with her ability to see the glory of the present. She was restless, always searching for the next fashion, trip, or job to make her happy. She chased after things because she had no present-day serenity with which to attract them. She was on overdrive, always justifying her frenzied pace by saying, "I'm just a perfectionist," or, "I'm a really intense person." She got so wrapped up in that role that only a dire medical event could slow her down.

Since her own thoughts focused on how much more she should

be doing or being, Kim also expected the same of everyone else. In other words, if she wasn't enough, you probably weren't either! Kim accomplished and acquired a lot of things but soon discovered that no matter where she ended up, it never felt like enough. She suffered physically, emotionally, and financially as a result.

It took two divorces and a trip to the emergency room with chest pains before she was willing to see that her attachment to future outcomes was making her life unmanageable. Ironically, her strenuous effort to control her future was the very thing preventing her from enjoying life.

There's a marvelous way to balance the scales of tomorrow and today—what I call the deal of a lifetime—and that's an attitude of gratitude. It costs nothing, you can't have too much of it, and it means everything to your future financial success.

Take A Minute:

When was the last time you took stock of what is going right in your life? How much you have accomplished? The great relationships you enjoy? The warmth of your home?

Don't worry: if it's been a while, that doesn't make you bad, just out of touch. Let's make sure that your basic financial thoughts include a celebration of the current gifts in your life.

- Take the next minute to write what you are so grateful for that the thought of it moves you emotionally. Here are some categories to help you:

    · Home
    · Family
    · Health
    · Opportunity
    · Friends
    · Talents
    · Time

_____

_____

_____

_____

_____

_____

_____

_____

_____

_____

Once you've made the list, look at it and ask yourself, "Is there anything in my life more important than this?" No matter how many challenges you face as you strive for financial success, you can always balance those concerns with the grateful perspective that says, "The good news is...."

Make A Minute:

Go back to the future. I promised you the present and the future could co-exist, as long as gratitude is present to temper your viewpoint.

- Choose ten things from your previous gratitude list that you're grateful for but would like to improve. For each one, write how you would like it to be and then write at least one action that you are willing to take to realize that improvement.

Example:

Area of Gratitude	What to improve	Action
My marriage	Share more intimate time with my partner	Have dining-room dinners at least once a week, no TV

Area of Gratitude	What to improve	Action
1.		
2.		
3.		
4.		
5.		
6.		
7.		
8.		
9.		
10.		

When you complete this assignment, go back and look at your action items. Do all of them involve spending more money? If so, go through them once again and choose actions that would cost nothing, or very little, to accomplish the same outcome.

Make Another Minute:

Go to *www.google.com* and type in "gratitude quotes". Surf the sites to find a meaningful quote to carry in your wallet, or write one of your own.

.
.

An attitude of gratitude needs cultivation to grow, so remember to engage in it daily by reading your list or adding to it. It is a sure-fire way to remind you that happiness comes in better form than by way of your wallet.

CHAPTER *five*

You're Enough
Without Your Stuff

:05 Remember the scene from *The Wizard of Oz* where Dorothy discovers that the great and powerful Oz is nothing more than a man behind a curtain with a microphone? She is so certain that he has the answers to her happiness, but finds they were within her all along.

What a perfect metaphor for the illusions of wealth that bombard us: we see common symbols of prosperity—homes, cars, jewelry, and clothes—and assume levels of health and happiness often completely contrary to reality. Worse, we don't use our assumptions as clues for success, as in "I wonder how I can get there?" Instead, we often use them as further proof of what we lack, telling ourselves "I'll never get there." I'm all for nice things, but in order to be truly content we must learn to derive more satisfaction from who we are than from what we have.

Think for a moment about the preconceived notions you might have about other people and their money. When you're on the highway and a striking person in a beautiful, new, convertible Mercedes Benz passes you, what goes through your mind? Do you make assumptions about the person? Perhaps you question the driver's character, assume they're superficial, that things mean more to them than people. What about the car? Do you envy the driver for it, perhaps long for one because of what owning it would say about you? Or do you just see an attractive person in a beautiful car?

Let's look at the flip side of this question. Instead of the Mercedes, let's say you're passed on the road by a car built in the 1970's, that's seen better days and driven by someone dressed very casually. Do you assume things about the driver's financial condition, wondering who would drive such a heap? Think about the decisions and judgments we make every day based on what we see or, more accurately, by what we think we see.

Looking back at our example, the Mercedes owner could be someone of comfortable means—or a person one payment away from bankruptcy. What about our friend in the older car? He could be a person who is down on his luck—or a multi-millionaire who views a car as merely a method of transportation. How do you know by looking? You don't, and you get nowhere by assuming.

Dan:

Dan was into having stuff—lots of stuff: cars, clothes, jewelry, trips, and fancy dinners. Dan didn't have money when he was growing up, so when he became an adult and started making lots of money, he felt it was his inalienable right to buy whatever he wanted, whatever made him feel good.

Unfortunately for Dan, he made most of his money during the dot-com boom and thought the ride on that gravy train would go on forever. Well, the train got derailed. Dan lost everything in the stock market crash of 2001. Worse than the loss of material things (and he lost a lot of things), Dan lost self esteem because he equated who he was with what he possessed. It took him a long time to separate his material attachments from his personal identity.

He persevered—spending hours upon hours on personal development—and discovered things about himself that brought him greater satisfaction than he had ever felt before. One of the things he learned while rebuilding financially was how to do things that, in his money-making days, he would have paid someone else to do—like repairing things around the house.

It turned out Dan had a great knack for fixing things in creative ways. That led him to start a handyman business, which brought renewed financial success. Careful not to let the money take center stage again, he has kept the moderate lifestyle that was once a matter of necessity, but which he came to enjoy, and has used his rising earnings to create security in the form of savings and investments.

To see him today, you would never know that he has the net-worth he does. He drives a modest car, wears nice, but inexpensive clothes and spends time enjoying the outdoors more with free hikes than with costly ski vacations. What you would know about him is what a warm, caring and personable man he is, because that's what he's made sure you'll notice.

Take A Minute:

Your challenge is to gauge how much of your self-worth is defined by what you accomplish or possess. To really live your best life, you need to delight in who you are apart from what you have or do.

- Make a list of ten of your most valuable possessions.
- Grade their worth, on a scale of one to ten, with ten indicating the greatest value to you.
- For each item use one adjective to describe the value that you receive from it.

Example: *Oil painting—Classy—9*

10 Most Valuable Possessions	Word to describe them	On a scale of 1 to 10, how much are they worth to me?
1.		
2.		
3.		

4.		
5.		
6.		
7.		
8.		
9.		
10.		

Make A Minute:

- Take the ten adjectives from above and use them in the next grid to describe you. On a scale from one to ten, how would you rate yourself in those terms?

Example: *Classy (me)—8*

10 Adjectives	On a scale of 1 to 10, how would I grade myself?	Action to improve my score
1.		
2.		
3.		
4.		
5.		

6.		
7.		
8.		
9.		
10.		

- Choose one action that would improve your score by at least two points. Even if you were a ten, what would it take for you to become a twelve?

Example: *Always speak well of others.*

This might feel awkward at first, because you may not be accustomed to paying yourself this kind of attention. Maybe the adjective you used for one of your objects doesn't represent a personal value for you. That's okay. Aim for a minimum of ten words to describe you that make you feel at least one degree better than the ones you use to describe your belongings.

⋮

Come back to this exercise often. The more you strengthen your sense of internal worth, the less dependent you are on externals to feel good, and the more you control those influences, the more you control your money.

CHAPTER *six*

Practice Makes Perfect

We're not responsible for what comes into our heads; we're responsible for what we do with it. —Anonymous

:06 In previous chapters we looked at deliberate acts of thought: examining your story, exercising faith, focusing on a new future, and generating gratitude. But what do you do with random ideas that oppose what you're trying to accomplish?

When negative thoughts come, they're often followed by more limiting thoughts, and if we let that continue, we create a spiral of pessimism that gets us nowhere. Even worse, our reactions can take us to a solution that is no solution at all—one that may set us back even further. However, if we teach ourselves to stop for a moment, to pause and look at things from different angles, we create a space where solutions can appear.

Where do you start? With a willingness to be curious: to challenge your thoughts first, and make your mind up about them later. As you investigate new thoughts about money, your old beliefs may rise up to fight the information because it doesn't fit what you think you know. You will overcome the tendency to drop back into old thought patterns when you learn to notice the resistance, stay curious, examine new angles of thought, and then decide your course of action. Too often we close viable avenues for growth with what's known as "contempt prior to investigation."

Examine the opening quote: "We're not responsible for what comes into our heads; we're responsible for what we do with it." That tells us we can't control what first comes into our minds, but that we have the choice to either react or respond to those thoughts.

Let's say your thought is: "I really should be saving for retirement." Your very next thought will be a statement or a question to answer the first thought. So your secondary thought will either be a reaction: "Why can't I make enough to make that happen?", or it will be a response: "How can I make enough money to make that happen?"

Being reactive means you're staying in the problem. In the example above, it means you won't save anything for retirement. But being responsive means being in the solution, which leads you to your answers.

Take A Minute:

In the following financial scenarios, test whether you react or respond. Be *really* honest because it won't help you create a wealthier future to pretend you feel other than you do.

- Read the next five statements. As soon as you've read one, write your immediate thought—not what you think you should feel about it.

I need to save for retirement.

_____

_____

I want to have money in savings.

_____

_____

I need to track my spending.

_____

_____

I need to figure out how to invest.

_____

_____

I want to make more money.

_____

_____

Look back at your answers. Do they represent any limiting thoughts? If the answer is yes for any of the five, take heart. All of us periodically struggle with our thoughts. The trick is to let our positive beliefs—rather than our negative ones—have the final word.

Make A Minute:

Here are three steps to get you to thoughts that serve you:

- **Step One: Get Curious**
  Take notice of what followed your original thought. Just notice, don't judge it. Say, "I'm curious. Where did that come from?"

- **Step Two: Examine the thought**
  Ask yourself, "How does this thought support me and how does it hold me back?"

- **Step Three: Find empowering alternatives**
  Ask yourself, "What's another way to look at this?" So if it's a limiting thought, look for an alternative. If it's a thought that already supports you, look for another one to go with it.

When you investigate other angles, you'll probably find several you hadn't thought of before. Keep asking the above question until you find a different or additional alternative that empowers you to take action.

Make Another Minute:

Go back to your answers to the original statements and go through each of these steps.

- Get curious and identify what initiated the reply.
- Examine it to see how it helps you or how it holds you back.
- Then ask yourself about the other ways you can look at the situation. Keep looking at different angles until you find one that will move you forward.

Response #1:

_____

Where does it come from?

_____

How does it help me?

_____

How does it hold me back?

_____

What's a different or additional way to look at it?

_____

Response #2:

_____

Where does it come from?

_____

How does it help me?

_____

How does it hold me back?

_____

What's a different or additional way to look at it?

_____

Response #3:

_____

Where does it come from?

_____

How does it help me?

_____

How does it hold me back?

_____

What's a different or additional way to look at it?

_____

Response #4:

_____

Where does it come from?

_____

How does it help me?

_____

How does it hold me back?

_____

What's a different or additional way to look at it?

_____

Response #5:

_____

Where does it come from?

_____

How does it help me?

_____

How does it hold me back?

_____

What's a different or additional way to look at it?

_____

⋮

Thoughts come into your mind at lightning speed, day in and day out, while you're asleep and while you're awake. You can't control them, but you can choose what you do with them. Get in the habit of challenging your thoughts by practicing these steps and you'll find more options and strategies for your life than you ever thought possible!

CHAPTER seven

Great Expectations

:07 Great Expectations—a dating service that was popular when I was in the industry—was based on matchmaking through video profiles. My dating service promoted a more personalized process. Many people who were successfully matched through our compatibility system told me they might not have chosen their partners if they had only seen video profiles. They told me that although physical attraction was necessary, it was ultimately more important to fit with their partners on other levels.

Great expectations were also what my clients brought with them as they searched for the love of their life—greatly unrealistic expectations, in many cases.

An interesting thing happened when these people stood up for what they really wanted. They sometimes overlooked the ways they needed to change because they were so focused on what should come from the other person.

In seven years with that service I counseled at least 2,000 people on attracting the right relationship. A large percentage of them had requirements in the list of traits they were looking for that they didn't personally embody: older men who were out of shape and looking for hard-bodied young women, or women with scant checkbooks of their own looking for a financially responsible man. Not all of them were that dramatically out of sync with what they desired, but many of them did hope to meet someone to fill in the blanks of what they lacked. However, the ones who experienced the most success were those who concentrated as much on what they had to offer as on what they sought. The same is true with money. Your financial success depends on bringing as much life and energy to your money as you envision it bringing to you.

:

The theory of attraction simply says we attract people, finances or circumstances that reflect what we think we're worth.

More specifically, attraction is the unseen magnet that draws people and circumstances to you because you're open, ready, and willing to accept them. It's being so sure you're involved in the right thing that others can't help but be drawn to you. It's an energy that causes a stir, not by being bigger or louder than everything else, but by its degree of confidence.

So, you attract who or what you are *being*—in love or in money, for better or for worse. I'm willing to bet that if you're reading this book, you're interested in attracting money to support what you love, whether that's your life partner, your work, or serving others. And nothing makes you more attractive than being happily involved with and honoring what matters to you most. That energy is what draws things to you with seemingly little effort.

Take A Minute:
- What are some of the great things you have attracted in your life?

_____

_____

_____

- What state of your being attracted them?

_____

_____

_____

Imagine the impact of showing up for all aspects of your life in a state of complete abundance, as though everything was already exactly as you'd like it. What could it mean for your occupation if you worked like you didn't need the money? What could it mean for your relationships with friends and family to show up with confidence and enthusiasm, in spite of the state of your checkbook?

Make A Minute:

Let's focus more specifically on your money:
- Write five things you want money to bring you—what you are most attracted to financially—be it free time, amusing experiences, or peace of mind.

What I want money to bring:

1. _____

2. _____

3. _____

4. _____

5. _____

Go back to each answer and write down one action you will take to create those circumstances now, regardless of your current financial state.

Example: Free time: I will free my time each day to enjoy the blessings in my life.

Action I will take to create the circumstances today:

1. _____

2. _____

3. _____

4. _____

5. _____

- Record the results. Don't just record them silently either—declare your victories out loud! Show others what happens when you change your mind and believe in life first, money second.

_____

_____

_____

_____

_____

.
.
.

To reap life's benefits, you have to be willing to bring to it what you seek. Focus on embodying the benefits first. If fun is something you want in your life, dedicate yourself to the principle of fun and it won't matter how much money you have, fun will find you. If peace of mind is your focus, you'll find peace of mind in all kinds of ways, not just financially.

John Wesley, founder of the Methodist church said, "Catch on fire with enthusiasm and people will come for miles to watch you burn." Do the same with your financial attraction—be abundant in your thoughts, language, and action and watch what comes to you. You'll be amazed by the opportunities that present themselves when you invite them.

CHAPTER eight

Back To The Future!

:08 I may not know you personally, but if you've done the exercises to this point, I know you've courageously looked at your financial patterns and been willing to change.

Now I want you to anchor what you've learned before you start expressing yourself in the next section.

Many congratulations for all that you've done to get to this point. I promise these shifts can support you for life.

Take A Minute:

In the space below, or in your journal, write what is different financially as a result of the work you've done.

Chapter One: Once Upon A Time ~ Writing a new story

_____

_____

_____

_____

Chapter Two: Have Faith ~ It's bigger than fear

_____

_____

_____

_____

Chapter Three: Ommmmm ~ Focus your faith

_____

_____

_____

_____

Chapter Four: Blue Light Special ~ Be grateful

_____

_____

_____

_____

Chapter Five: You're Enough Without Your Stuff ~ Choosing Self-worth before net-worth

_____

_____

_____

_____

Chapter Six: Practice Makes Perfect ~ Get curious

_____

_____

_____

_____

Chapter Seven: Great Expectations ~ Laws of Attraction

_____

_____

_____

_____

For this chapter, Back To The Future, write a vision for your financial future. Write it in present tense, as though you're already there. Include your state of being, how you feel, what has come to you from these changes, and how you've impacted others.

_____

_____

_____

_____

Make A Minute:

Celebrate! You've come a long way, so it's time to acknowledge a job well done. Find a simple but meaningful way to celebrate what you've done to this point.

Possibilities:

· Give yourself a hug or a literal pat on the back.
· Spread your arms wide, lift your face to the sky, and say thank you.
· Call someone and share your success.

PART two

WHAT DO YOU *say?*

CHAPTER nine

Watch Your Language

:09 You've built a new vision of financial success. When you share it with others, will your words match what's in your mind? What we think about our financial destiny goes a long way toward realizing it. What we say about it has just as much impact because it shows the rest of the world what vision to participate in.

This section develops language skills for financial success, ensuring that you articulate your goals in a way that leaves no one guessing. In later chapters we'll explore how to communicate your wants and needs, what affordability means, and the best way to talk about a budget. Now we're going to concentrate on what you say about yourself and your place in the world. You need a strong personal identity with which to support your financial future, because you'll only have as much of anything as your self-esteem allows.

So who are you? What do you absolutely know is true and wonderful about you?

I know it's tough to brag about yourself, but it's critical to your success for the world to experience your confidence. I'm not talking about being arrogant because that's never attractive. I'm talking about expressing, with conviction, who you are and your mission in life.

Take A Minute:

In Chapter 5, you separated your self-worth from your net-worth by grading each, and improving your personal scores over the material ones. This exercise takes things one step further by connecting your self-worth to your worth in the world.

- Start by writing five "I am...." statements that tell me who you are. Make them about your being, not your doing. So instead of saying, "I am a good mother," which is about something you do, tell me the essence of what makes you a good mother. For example, "I am deeply caring."

If you're not sure about your positive attributes, ask two friends or family members for input. Still not sure? Here's a list from which to choose, submitted by clients and friends:

Athletic	Friendly	Magnetic
Brash	Frugal	Majestic
Caring	Fun-loving	Opinionated
Chatty	Generous	Passionate
Clever	Genuine	Personable
Coachable	Grateful	Playful
Committed	Hard-working	Present
Competitive	Honest	Prissy
Confident	Humorous	Resourceful
Connector	Intelligent	Respectful
Content	Intuitive	Sassy
Courageous	Inventive	Sensitive
Creative	Independent	Serious
Curious	Innocent	Strategic
Decisive	Innovative	Tenacious
Dependable	Insightful	Thoughtful
Direct	Knowing	Tolerant
Focused	Loving	Zealous

You will know what words best describe you because of the emotional charge that comes with picking them. If you tingle a little, maybe even feel a little shy about a choice, chances are you're on to something.

I am:

1. _____

2. _____

3. _____

4. _____

5. _____

Put a checkmark by the two characteristics that best describe you. We'll come back to them in a minute.

Take Another Minute:

Now let's talk about your life's mission:

- Pretend I'm Oprah, and you have an opportunity to tell me about your life's purpose. Use your journal or computer, the space below or tell it to a tape recorder, but take five minutes to tell me what you want your life to mean.

_____

_____

_____

_____

_____

_____

_____

_____

_____

_____

- Now go back and look at or listen to what you said. Is there any limiting language? Here are four words or phrases to look for that can subtly sabotage your success:

"just" ~ "kind of" ~ "maybe" ~ "actually"

- Take out the words that make you sound unsure, and re-state your life's purpose until it's strong and decisive. Keep working until you can boil your mission down to a sentence or two.

Your Personal Mission:

_____

_____

_____

_____

_____

Here's mine:
My life is about discovering, developing and delighting in my God-given talents, for the sake of personal growth and impact on others.

Here's what it used to sound like:
I just hope to find something someday I could actually like about me, and maybe find a way to help other people too.

Pretty different, yes? Now, remember your Money Mantra from the first section? It's time to create your Personal Power Statement, the declaration of who you are combined with your life's mission.

Make A Minute:
- Take your two favorite traits, the ones you checked above, and combine them with your mission statement to create your Personal Power Statement.

As an example, my friend and client, Linda, says of herself:

I am endowed with great humor and compassion, and am destined to make a difference in the world!

My combined statement is:

I am dedicated to using my intuition and focus for the sake of personal growth and impact on others.

Your Personal Power Statement:

_____

_____

_____

_____

_____

Make Another Minute:

- Write your Personal Power Statement on something you can easily carry with you, perhaps in the same place you wrote your Money Mantra.
- Commit and schedule time to focus on it—maybe combine it with meditating on your Money Mantra.
- Record the changes that result from this focus.

_____

_____

_____

_____

_____

_____

_____

_____

.
.
.

Your words affect the opportunities that come to you. Greater opportunities bring greater financial rewards. So know your positive qualities and intentions and how to declare them, and watch what comes from that confidence.

CHAPTER ten

The $64,000 Question

:10 Can I afford it?

In one two-week span, the subject of affordability surfaced around me no less than thirty times. In 95% of the conversations, the only gauge for affordability was whether there was money to accommodate the desire. The answer to the question the majority of the time was a resounding, "No." At least twenty-eight times I heard people say they couldn't be, do, or have something, because the money wasn't there—including a ten-year-old boy who already thought he had only one choice for college because of what Mom said they could afford. How will it shape this young boy's life if he's left to believe that people are only as capable as their checkbooks allow?

You're bound to confront this subject as you create the life of purpose and intention you're exploring, so let's look at whether you're limiting your opportunities by using the state of your finances as the deciding factor in affordability.

Take A Minute:

- List three things you want, but tell yourself you can't afford, things that on a scale from one to ten are at least an eight in their level of importance. One might be a professional opportunity, like growing your business, or something material, like a piano or a car.

I can't afford to:

1. _____

2. _____

3. _____

Example:

A client named Cindy said:

> *I can't afford to start my own business.*

Now write down why you think you can't afford to have the things you listed.

1.
_____
_____

2.
_____
_____

3.
_____
_____

Example:

Cindy's answer:

> *I can't afford to lose my regular income during the time it would take to build something new.*

Cindy's reasoning in this example was true—she was not in a financial position to abandon her current income to start a new business. But she was allowing this rationale to signal the end of the line for her plan to be a business owner. She wanted to be coached on how to resolve the conflict because it tortured her to think that money would have the last word in how she planned her life.

In order to move forward with her idea she needed to figure out if there were bigger questions to ask herself about the situation. I asked her, "Is it a question of whether you *want* a business or whether you can afford to abruptly leave your job to start a business?" She definitely wanted her own business for the time it would allow her with her kids.

By answering the main question of whether or not she really wanted a business, and why she wanted it, she went from agonizing over why she couldn't do it to strategizing how she could. She used that determination to figure out how to transition from working a job to opening a business and eventually opened a kid's camp that met all her goals, including the financial ones. Had she stayed focused on an either/or solution she would have shut down a brilliant idea based solely on whether she could bear the cost.

.
.
.

What we really need to know when we ask ourselves if we can afford something is:

Can we afford the consequences of bringing it into our lives?
Does it support the bigger picture to have it in our lives?

The quality of our lives is determined by the quality of the questions we ask ourselves, so maybe a better question concerning affordability is:

Does it make sense *for me to have/do/be "x"?*

Based on the work you did in the last chapter, you could also frame that to say,

Does it support me and my mission (as stated in your Personal Power Statement) to have/do/be "x"?

Make A Minute:

- Open up to the bigger question of what you're trying to accomplish.

Let's say it's a piano you want, and have told yourself you can't afford because you don't have the money. The first question isn't, "Can I afford a piano?" It's, "Why do I want a piano?" If it's for the sake of general amusement, maybe it goes on hold until you save up the money. If becoming a concert pianist is your one, true aim in life then it's time you had a piano and got creative about how to make that happen.

- Take each of your examples and identify the real question, which is, "Why do I want this...."

#1:

What I want: _____

Why I want it:

_____

_____

#2:

What I want: _____

Why I want it:

_____

_____

#3:

What I want: _____

Why I want it:

_____

_____

Then, for each of these, ask yourself:

What needs to be in place for this to make sense?

This could mean resources, money, or people, so list everything you think it would take to realize your goal. Then look at those components and truthfully assess whether you're committed enough to the goal to make it happen.

#1:

What do I want? _____

Why do I want it? _____

What needs to be in place for it to make sense?

_____

_____

_____

_____

_____

Do I want it badly enough to make it happen? _____

#2:

What do I want? _____

Why do I want it? _____

What needs to be in place for it to make sense?

_____

_____

_____

_____

_____

Do I want it badly enough to make it happen? _____

#3:

What do I want? _____

Why do I want it? _____

What needs to be in place for it to make sense?

_____

_____

_____

_____

_____

_____

Do I want it badly enough to make it happen? _____

Re-cap:
- What do you say you can't afford?
- Why do you say you can't afford it?
- Why do you want it? How would having this support who you are and what you want your life to be about?
- What needs to be in place for it to make sense?
- Are you still committed to it?

These questions can be asked as easily about a trip to the mall as they can about your lifelong goals. You'll know whether you're fooling yourself about having something or whether it really supports you when you take that extra moment to examine how it fits in with everything else.

.
.
.

Don't close the door on opportunities by narrowing your definition of affordability to mean only the price tag. Affordability is a matter of desire, and identifying a high level of desire is one of the most important criteria for living the life of your dreams.

CHAPTER eleven

Wants Vs. Needs

:11 When it comes to spending money, many people get caught in the exhausting debate of "want versus need" by trying to justify one over the other. It's tough determining which is which, right?

Wrong. Let me simplify this: we purchase things because we want them, because they meet a need for us. So there's really no difference between the two. Make sense? Everything that's in our life is there because we saw a need for it when we bought it. What we really want to discover is what need we're trying to meet, and whether the purchase is the best solution for meeting it. Having needs is okay—we just need to create the means to meet them with something other than our wallets.

A certain consciousness on our part—a definition for the word need and a system of choosing an appropriate response to the need—gives us the flexibility to take care of ourselves and protect our cash flow.

Randall:

Randall and I first started working on his budget (a word we'll get into next chapter) because his cash flow suffered each month despite a sizeable salary he received as a lawyer. While examining his income and expenses, I noticed a substantial line item for golf. When I asked him what the money paid for each month he said lessons, equipment, and play. His goal in spending that amount was to decrease his handicap by 5 strokes.

I asked him why that was important to him, expecting to hear something about friendly competition with his friends or a lifelong goal to have a single-digit handicap. Instead, he told me in great detail how a more proficient game would help him gain entry to private country clubs, and the opportunity the associations with its members would provide for his children—his unborn children at the time of our conversation. Heck, his un-conceived children at that point.

He was pinning the hopes of future generations on a five-point shift in his golf game. I told him I wasn't sure how he could even hit the ball with that kind of pressure! And at the rate he was spending to gain access to those perceived privileges, he could have funded several Ivy League educations, which would probably have made a more predictable difference to his children's future.

We examined the situation further to determine what was driving his decision to spend money this way. Randall said he wanted to see himself, and be seen by others, as someone who was a great provider for the kids he was sure he would have. So while he was out swinging the club and demonstrating his golf skill, he was also talking about what he planned for his family. We looked at other ways to achieve that sense of importance, and he decided that even though an improvement in his golf handicap would show an aptitude for the game, a growing savings account would be better proof of his ability to provide.

Randall wasn't off-base in wanting to provide for his kids or be recognized, just in his method for doing so in relation to how he wanted things to be financially. By reallocating some of the golf money to a savings account, he created a new option for meeting his need for security and significance, and relieved the financial stress of the one scenario he had been living with.

Take A Minute:

- Find a working definition for the word "need."

One that works for me is: "What I *must* have to be my best." My best at what? Let's take a professional example:

In my profession, I need to be impeccably dressed. That includes the shoes I put on my feet. They need to be certain things—polished, in style—but do they *need* to be $350 Prada's? No. Can you see the distinction?

- What is your definition of "need?"

_____

_____

_____

_____

_____

_____

- How will your definition of "need" help you make better financial choices?

_____

_____

_____

_____

_____

_____

Make A Minute:

Let's figure out what you need to be your best.

This exercise clarifies your needs in five major areas of your life. Start with these four, and then we'll apply this to the fifth category, which are your financial needs.

I need to...	Mentally	Emotionally	Physically	Spiritually
Be				
Do				
Be remembered for				

Fill in each block. Use the word in the left row and then finish the sentence with the word in the top column.

For instance, "I need to be mentally _____." Fill in the first block with how you want to see yourself in that category.

What are the activities that fulfill who you need to be mentally? Fill in the "Do" block with these answers. Then fill in how you want to be remembered in that way, how you want others to see you.

In my case, I need to see myself as one who is mentally stimulating, well read, and thought provoking. To support that, I read, research new ideas, and participate in a book club. I want to be remembered as someone who challenged herself mentally by learning new things.

Fill in the information for each of the categories.

Make Another Minute:

- Once you're clear about what you really need, list five ways you can meet those needs, from free to fee.

So in my example of mental needs, I meet those needs by being part of a book club, I do Internet research, and I borrow books from the library, all of which cost next to nothing. Sometimes I take classes, which can cost from around $25 on up. By doing this part of the exercise, I see that I have choices about how to meet the need, no matter what my bank account looks like!

Five Ways, From Free to Fee, to Meet My Needs:

	Mentally	Emotionally	Physically	Spiritually
1.				
2.				
3.				
4.				
5.				

Now do the exercise for your financial needs. By the time you get here, you've freed up all kinds of money that was previously getting spent to meet other needs. Decide how you want to *be* financially, what to do to make that happen, and how you want to be remembered.

I need to...	Financially
Be	
Do	
Be remembered for	

For this category, instead of free to fee, write five ways you can meet your financial needs using anything from a little money to a lot.

Five Ways, From a Little to a Lot, to Meet My Financial Needs:

1.
2.
3.
4.
5.

⋮

Remember, if you can determine what your needs are and develop a variety of options for meeting them, you will free yourself and your money!

CHAPTER twelve

What's In A Word?

:12 What happens to you when I say the word "budget?" Do you recoil in horror? I know I'm being dramatic. I also know this budget idea—what to call it, whether to have one, and how to have one—is another area where we hold ourselves back financially, starting with our resistance to the word itself.

What is it about the word "budget" that tortures us so? Many people have shared with me that a budget is about what they can't do, can't have, or did wrong. If you've gone any length of time spending money casually (or carelessly) and found yourself in trouble then you're right, having a budget probably seems like another indicator of your inability to manage. It's a lesson in self-torture to have a budget that is nothing more than a backward look at what's gone wrong.

If, however, you changed your mind about what a budget means, would you be more motivated to have one? Rather than completely backing away from the concept of a budget, learn to embrace the word's original intent, which is to plan or project how to direct your money to its greatest use. To put it more simply, change the word or change your mind about the word, but have the process intended by the word.

Take A Minute:

Let's examine your reaction to the word "budget".

- List five negative associations you have to the word "budget":

1. _____

2. _____

3. _____

4. _____

5. _____

- Now, using an exercise of opposites, write down what you would prefer it to mean.

Original meaning

1. _____

2. _____

3. _____

4. _____

5. _____

New meaning

1. _____

2. _____

3. _____

4. _____

5. _____

Review what you've written and choose to either change your mind about what the word "budget" means, or pick a new word or phrase with which to replace it. In the end, use whatever word or meaning for "budget" that will compel you to actually have one. Give yourself credit for deciding to see a budget in a better light; take time to feel the power of choosing a more optimistic thought process around it.

.
.

Many people assume that budgets only exist to keep an eye on things when money is in short supply. The most successful people in the world budget too, but their budget is a tracking device for the wonderful life they've decided is their right to live. You have that same right, so decide to have a budget for the sake of forecasting your fabulous future!

CHAPTER thirteen

Neither A Borrower Nor A Lender Be...Right?

:13 There are certain money messages that have followed us since the dawn of time. Whoever started them probably meant well, and people who live by them today might think they have good reasons for doing so, but you have to be careful not to buy into the ones that don't serve you.

By now you're accustomed to examining alternative thoughts and language with money, but these time-honored statements can be so subtly ingrained that you may not realize you're thinking or saying them. Let's take a look at some common examples to see if there are still hidden messages that hold you back in your financial choices.

"Neither a borrower nor a lender be."

Tom's story was the inspiration for this chapter. He had heard this message all his life, and it was keeping him from taking the next step with his consulting business.

Tom had meticulous details about the next phases of growth in his business, including a plan for how much money he needed, what it would pay for, and the marketing strategy to turn a profit. In spite of all this planning, he found he was unable to actually ask anyone for the money.

As with so many situations, a simple shift in perception generated a big change in action. Tom's shift came from looking at the difference between asking people to lend him money for the business and asking them to invest.

Lending carried a condition of return. Tom wasn't completely certain he could pay someone back, so he didn't feel good about asking someone to lend the money. Investors, however, commit without those conditions, knowing full well the risks involved. Allowing someone to take a chance on his business by becoming an investor freed him to see it in a whole new light—as one worth investing in, rather than just something to fund.

"Money doesn't grow on trees."

Barbara heard this repeatedly from her father regarding people's spending behavior, most of which he believed to be unwise. So Barbara learned she'd better not spend money on anything that wasn't important, because more would be hard to come by.

Consequently, she was overly cautious with money, rarely indulging in even the smallest luxuries.

She wanted to see the world as a beautiful, abundant place, but this money message opposed that. So Barbara adopted a new phrase—"Abundance is...."—a purposely open-ended statement that prompted her to lift the restrictions in her mind of what was financially possible. It helped her paint a picture in her mind of a world where all her needs were met, including the occasional manicure or massage. She continues to be financially responsible, but now includes self-care in that practice.

"Money is the root of all evil."

This one comes from the Bible, and as such, carries a very strong charge for some people. The problem is, that isn't the whole sentence. The original sentence begins: "For the *love* of money is the root of all evil...." (Timothy 6:10 KJV). There's an important distinction to be made with this message: the root of the problem is the idolization of money, not money itself.

Because money is so intertwined with things like corruption and greed—things we associate with evil—it is easy to conclude that one equals the other. But that unfairly excludes all the good that money does, like charity or growth of industry. Rather than shift the blame, we need to take personal responsibility for the evil or good that results from what we do with money.

"I don't....", "I can't...."

Then there are the seemingly insignificant, but very powerful messages we make up on our own about our financial ability. For example, have you ever been known to say, "I don't carry cash, I'll just spend it," or, "I can't be trusted at (fill in the blank with your favorite store); I never come out with what I went in for." We program our minds, by consistently repeating tiny phrases like these, to believe that we just can't control our financial destiny.

Take A Minute:

- What do you say about money that holds you back?

_____

_____

_____

_____

_____

- What do you say about money that supports you?

_____

_____

_____

_____

_____

Make A Minute:

- Take several days to record what people say about money that helps or hinders their cause. How could you rewrite what they've said to better suit your own circumstances?

_____

_____

_____

_____

_____

⋮

We strongly affect the chain of financial events in our lives by what we say out loud about money. For this reason, the one phrase that can always help you is: "Think before you speak."

CHAPTER *fourteen*

Dollars & Sense

:14 Every day we're bombarded by requests to spend money. As you discovered earlier, once you're clear about what you're trying to accomplish financially, you are less likely to get sucked in by these forces. Those bright, shiny objects just don't hold the same power over you. But it can still be tricky translating this resolve to others.

Is there any sentence more complete, more comprehensible than "No."? There is a special freedom in understanding that when you say "no," you don't need to clarify it. Brief explanations can go a long way in teaching people what you mean by "no," but you don't have to rationalize your decision. You simply need to stay committed to your financial goals and teach people how to take you seriously in the process.

Michelle:

Michelle was the go-to girl in her office whenever a party needed to be arranged. She enjoyed the responsibility, but fronting the money for each event got her in trouble. She needed to learn to say "no" to organizing those activities until she knew the budget and had the cash in hand. Otherwise, she would continue to find herself on the short end of the financial stick.

Here's what used to happen:

> **Boss:** Michelle, will you plan Katie's going-away party for next Friday?
> **Michelle:** Sure, how will we pay for that?
> **Boss:** Just take care of it, and we'll reimburse you from everyone's contributions.
> **Michelle:** Okay.

Michelle set out with a plan for the party first, paid to pull it together, and then gathered money. People contributed only what they felt like, and that usually left Michelle paying for a bigger share. She was afraid to ask her boss for reimbursement. After all, shouldn't she have figured it out correctly to begin with?

In a coaching session, we role-played a new conversation. Here's what it sounded like:

> **Boss:** Michelle, will you plan Katie's going-away party for next Friday?
> **Michelle:** Sure, how much would you like to spend on it?
> **Boss:** Just take care of it, and we'll reimburse you from everyone's contributions.
> **Michelle:** No, because if I pay for it first and then collect the money I get left paying a bigger share. Why don't we take up a collection first, let everyone contribute what makes sense for them, then plan accordingly?

Michelle learned to stand up for what was reasonable for her finances, and also set an example for others to do the same. Rather than expecting people to do things that didn't fit their budget, she encouraged everyone in the office to participate in a way that felt good for them.

Take A Minute:

- List five scenarios that challenge your ability to say "no."

1. _____

2. _____

3. _____

4. _____

5. _____

Make A Minute:

- Using the language you've learned about affordability, needs, and budgeting, practice saying "no" in those situations. We're not assuming you'll always need to say "no," just preparing you for the times you do.

Example:

"Can you contribute twenty dollars for a gift for Susie?"

No, that doesn't make sense for my budget right now, but I'm happy to give you ten dollars—will that help?

1.

_____

_____

2.

_____

_____

3.

_____

_____

4.

_____

_____

5.

_____

_____

•
•

Congratulations for taking a verbal stand to support your financial success. Celebrate the next time you say "no" when saying "yes" would have set you back.

CHAPTER fifteen

Mind Your Manners

:15 As we work on changing our financial circumstances, we change too, usually by becoming more self-assured and improving our surroundings. Other people typically acknowledge these differences with a general compliment. What happens when someone offers you praise? Do you simply say "thank you," or instantly find yourself downplaying what prompted the admiring comment?

Besides just being good manners, responding courteously to congratulations keeps you aligned with all the other principles of abundance you've learned. For instance, can you be truly grateful for your financial rewards if you can't express that gratitude verbally? Can you enjoy the greatest self-esteem if you hold it in your mind but don't recognize it aloud?

It doesn't support your vision of financial freedom to set goals, and go after and achieve them just to halt all that great energy by justifying or apologizing for your good fortune. In order to use the principles of new financial thought and language most success-fully, and further the flow of abundance, you must teach yourself to graciously accept praise and give thanks.

Julie:

Julie did not know how to accept a compliment. She grew up believing that success was something reserved for everyone but her. She went out of her way to prove it by not taking care of herself physically, emotionally, or financially.

Working with Julie was challenging. She wanted to clean up her finances, but she didn't want to hear that changing her outlook on life would help balance her checkbook. She spent most of our time together beating herself up and dismissed even small compliments with reasons why she wasn't good enough.

I told her what it felt like to be rejected that way, to constantly have my opinions about her rebuffed. I shared how difficult it was to help when I felt constantly pushed away. What really got her attention was telling her I wouldn't work with her if it was always going to be a fight, that I wasn't interested in spending all my time defending my opinions. She had never considered that her behavior was holding off the very help she wanted; her focus had only been on herself, on the discomfort of accepting a compliment.

She agreed to become more respectful of other's opinions, not to necessarily instantly agree with them, but to at least honor the other person's right to have them. In time she gave herself permission to be liked, which directly contributed to her professional advancement by making her easier to get to know, and therefore, easier to promote. She made more friends, grew her professional network, and gradually started to see what others saw in her.

She made room to believe she was worthy of peace by her willingness to believe she was worthy of praise. She used that shift in perception as motivation to pay better attention to her money. The more she learned to trust that she had great qualities, the less time she spent testing your theories about that: she became less self-centered and more interested in using her experiences to grow and help others.

Take A Minute:

- What do you apologize for?

_____

_____

_____

- Why do you apologize for it?

_____

_____

_____

- Who or what are you rejecting by not accepting compliments?

_____

_____

_____

- How is that affecting your financial position?

_____

_____

_____

Make A Minute:

- Spend one week just saying "thank you" when someone acknowledges the good in you—no explanations allowed—and record the results from that.

_____

_____

_____

_____

_____

⋮

One last word on the subject of giving thanks: what if our enthusiasm for the progress in our lives is just the charge someone needs to jump-start their own goals? I'm not talking about being conceited about our accomplishments, but about sharing the happiness from recognizing our rewards so that others are more encouraged to find and appreciate their rewards. Look at thanks as a gift to someone: a way to affect the cycle of abundance for them as well as for you.

CHAPTER *sixteen*

The Energy Of Money

:16 When we flip the switch on the wall it sends energy through the wire to give us what we need—in this case, light. Money is energy too—why do you think they call it currency? Everything in the book to this point has been about preparing the conduits—our thoughts and our words—to carry the energy of money to light up the values of our life.

You have accessed many energy sources in your search for financial freedom: powerful thoughts, stronger language, certain values, and definitive communication. Plug in to this immense grid of solutions on a regular basis and before you know it, you'll have more energy for your goals than you know what to do with!

Let's outline what has changed for you from the work you've done in this section before we move into action in the next one.

Take A Minute:

Look at the aim of each chapter, and record the changes that have occurred by adapting these strategies. Review who you were in the past and who you are now by aligning yourself with these principles.

Chapter Nine: Watch Your language ~ Empower yourself

Then—

_____

_____

Now—

_____

_____

Chapter Ten: The $64,000 Question ~ Affordability

Then—

_____

_____

Now—

_____

_____

Chapter Eleven: Wants Vs. Needs ~ Choosing your options

Then—

_____

_____

Now—

_____

_____

Chapter Twelve: What's In A Word? ~ Having a budget

Then—

_____

_____

Now—

_____

_____

Chapter Thirteen: Neither A Borrower... ~ Money messages

Then—

_____

_____

Now—

_____

_____

Chapter Fourteen: Dollars & Sense ~ How to say "no"

Then—

_____

_____

Now—

_____

_____

Chapter Fifteen: Mind Your Manners ~ How to say "thank you"

Then—

_____

_____

Now—

_____

_____

Chapter Sixteen: The Energy Of Money ~ Plug in regularly

Then—

_____

_____

Now—

_____

_____

Make A Minute:

- Arm yourself for the actions to come with a simple declaration of intent:

May my financial actions speak louder than my thoughts or words.

⋮

What an amazing feeling it is to know that a different financial destiny can be created by what you think and say about money. Combine these thoughts and words with the practical action steps in the next section, and you'll have the freedom from financial worry you've always wanted.

PART three

WHAT DO YOU *do?*

CHAPTER *seventeen*

Budget Your Balance

:17 You embraced the idea of a budget in Chapter 12, and in the next chapter you will outline one. This chapter directs you to which areas of personal fulfillment to include in your budget. You've heard the expression, "All work and no play makes Jack a dull boy"? The same is true here: budgeting your personal development with your other financial obligations helps you maintain your motivation for all of it.

We talked about the "gotta's" of the typical budget—gotta pay the mortgage, gotta keep the lights on, gotta see that Johnny plays soccer. But what about you? Where do you figure in it? How do you take care of yourself?

In Chapter 11, you developed five ways, from free to fee, to meet your emotional, mental, physical, spiritual, and financial needs. Now you'll choose which of them in each category to budget for. We'll determine the result you're after and how much it costs. Then, when you're working with your budget, you'll decide how to finance it. You can use this strategy of articulating your ultimate outcome to pinpoint any goal.

Deciding the Outcome:

This is the simplest exercise I know for deciding what result you want for any given goal. I developed this after spending lots of time with great motivational systems from Anthony Robbins® and Franklin-Covey® where they teach you how to connect emotionally to an outcome and map it out, but not necessarily how to articulate the outcome in the first place. So this gets you focused on what you want to experience in your goal, not just where you want to end up. You can do this even if you're just trying to budget time instead of money.

⋮

We'll use something from the list of ways to meet my mental needs, as an example of how to use the exercise. The example will be:

Take a week-long painting trip in France.

Looking at that statement, is the trip itself really the goal? I probably have more to the experience in my mind, like desiring the city or the country, meeting many people or just a few, painting outdoors or in—you get the point. So in order to decide my true outcome, I simply start by making a list of eight to ten things I want.

Example:
What do I want?
1. Small group—no more than twelve
2. Individual instruction
3. Landscapes as well as architecture to paint
4. Watercolor instruction
5. More than one city to visit
6. Great food
7. Decent accommodations
8. $5000 or less in expenses
9. One week long

Then I make a list of what I don't want.

What don't I want?

1. More than twelve people
2. Too busy an agenda
3. Too many cities
4. Bad hotels
5. No time to sightsee
6. No alone time
7. More than $5000 in expenses

Now, we never get 100% of what we want, or avoid 100% of what we don't, but by deciding what our top three priorities are in each list, we get closer to our real goal. So, we go back to each list, and pick the top three details to have and the top three to avoid, and we do so by categorizing them as the "must-have's" and the "deal-killers."

So, in my example, the top three "must haves" are:

1. Small group
2. Watercolor class
3. $5000 or less in expenses

My "deal-killers" are:

1. No alone time
2. Too many cities
3. Bad hotels

I got to these by looking at each item on the do's and don't's lists and asking myself questions like,

Must *I have this to enjoy the experience?*

Must *it be a dream-come-true trip?*

Between this and this, which is most *important?*

Is this just a nice detail, or is it the reason I want to go?

Once I've gotten to these top criteria, I can create an outcome statement, which in this case is:

To spend a week in the French countryside with an intimate group of people, studying watercolor, sharing food and enjoying the local sights, for $5000 or less.

The next step is to start researching the details of when I'd like to go, ways to get there, classes being offered that fit my description and all the costs involved. As you know, one of my favorite research tools is Google™ on the Internet. I went there and put in the keywords, "watercolor class France", and about a third of the way down the first page, I came up with a trip that matched my description.

Once I find a way to accomplish my outcome, I can decide how I want to budget for it, including a timeframe in which to pay for it.

You may not know what you do and don't want from an experience because you've never done anything like it before. So you might start with a smaller version of it like, in this case, a day-long watercolor class instead of a week in France. You're not risking as much time and money this way and you can be more open to what you do and don't want while you go through it.

The next few chapters will address ways to accomplish your financial goals creatively. The point here is to focus first on what you want from the experience, then we'll move on to how to get it.

Take A Minute:
- Choose an avenue of personal fulfillment to budget for.
- Make a list of eight to ten things you do and do not want from the experience.
- Choose the top three "must-have's" and the top three "deal-killers" from each list.
- Use those to create your ultimate outcome statement.

Avenue of fulfillment:

_____

_____

_____

What do I want?

1. _____
2. _____
3. _____
4. _____
5. _____
6. _____
7. _____
8. _____
9. _____
10. _____

What don't I want?

1. _____
2. _____
3. _____
4. _____
5. _____
6. _____
7. _____
8. _____
9. _____
10. _____

Top three "must-have's"

1. _____
2. _____
3. _____

Top three "deal-killers"

1. _____

2. _____

3. _____

Ultimate Outcome Statement:

_____

_____

_____

_____

_____

Make A Minute:

- Go online to research ways to meet your outcome.
- Decide on a scenario to budget for.

_____

_____

_____

_____

_____

_____

.
.

How much more motivated will you be to have a budget when it's about more than just the basics? Doing this work will not only let you rise into a bigger vision for your life, but also give you tools to teach others to do the same. Imagine having your whole family committed to a life of greater potential, *and* creating the means to get there!

CHAPTER *eighteen*

Call In The Troops

:18 No great fight is fought alone, and there's no better time than now to enlist help as you detail the finances behind the life of your dreams.

It's time to create a comprehensive outline of your financial obligations and get the key people in your life involved in the process.

A quick word on that subject:

If you and a partner are already working together to organize the family finances, bravo! That will go a long way toward the realization of your goals. If you're the sole financial manager in the relationship, don't despair: you may assume the main responsibility of charting your family's financial course, but still encourage them to be involved.

If you're going it alone, or are single, find some means of support. A coach can be very effective, or a group of friends who want to apply these principles and keep one another accountable. In any case, you'll greatly increase your chances for success by working in tandem with like-minded people.

If "money manager" is a new role for you, you might be challenged in convincing others of your financial change of heart. Some will treat it as though it were a religious conversion, so be mindful of overwhelming them with unbridled zeal. Go easy, but be secure in the knowledge that you're doing the right thing by being the agent of change.

When you work with others, keep an open mind about how to budget successfully. Studies show that collaboration, or the co-creating of goals, brings about lasting change. So be open to new methods while keeping your focus on the result of creating a complete financial map.

Putting your budget on paper involves effort, so don't get discouraged if it takes more than one meeting to complete. What's most important is to take your time, be thorough, and, if working in a group, give others the chance to do the same.

Take Several Minutes:

You decided many chapters ago whether your outline will be called a budget, a spending plan, or something else. For our purposes, I will refer to it as a budget. The goal is to detail your income and expenses and see where you stand.

Here's what you'll need:
- Pens/Paper/Budget forms (see Appendix A or download a budget form from the Internet)
- Bills—upcoming and recent past (the last three months should do)
- Credit card statements—three months worth
- Bank statements—three months worth
- Check registers—three months worth
- Investment statements—if you're receiving income from them. (We won't be addressing net-worth here. For excellent books on the subject, see the Resources section.)

There are lots of forms to use for budgeting, including the one I've included in the Appendix. Add whatever spaces you need to cover income and expenses not already included on the form.

Fill in the budget form with averages of the information from the bills and statements you've gathered.

Don't forget to budget for the personal goals you worked on in the last chapter. You may decide to include them as a one-time expense or divide the costs into several months.

Also, think about what's coming up in terms of celebrations, and estimate the costs involved for travel, food or gifts.

Be sure to include a savings or investment goal in your budget. You can get more specific about what this needs to look like once you've met with a financial planner. So, if you're not clear on how much to budget for, just guess for now.

Brainstorm as long as you need to, even if it takes additional meetings, until you're satisfied that you've covered all your bases for income and expenses.

Make A Few More Minutes:

- Get the bottom line of your budget by balancing your expenses against your income.

You may be in the negative, based on your current situation. Take a deep breath and understand that the next two chapters will help you develop strategies to increase your income and decrease your expenses to help you meet your goals.

⋮

What if your family or friends don't want to participate? Can you follow through on budgeting and planning, if only for your own sake? I'm not suggesting this would be easy, but you have to look at the alternatives. If you go back to doing what you've done, where will it take you? Can you live with those consequences? Maybe there are other ways to bring family around.

Consider this possibility: you're in control of managing the family finances, and no one else wants to cooperate. You can start raising their interest by restricting access, if only verbally at first. Let's say your teenager wants something and is used to getting his or her way. Normally, your response would be to say "yes" while you scramble around to find the money. You've now tried to get your teenager involved with the family budget, but something else always comes up. This time, respond to their request by saying, "I don't see that happening right now and if you'd like to know why, we can sit down and discuss the details." Lots of people will make the time when their individual interests are at stake.

If you're not in control of any household finances and the party in charge won't let you anywhere near them, bigger problems may be afoot—it might be time to get your own checking account!

For the most part, family and friends want you to be happy. Simply say the word, and they'll be there for you. Even children will step up to the plate when they know it's important. Children under seven may not be ready for the adult nature of the budgeting conversation, but they can still play a part. They can be official phone answerers (if they've been taught how) to keep the peace while the family meeting is in progress. They can be dog watchers or room guards or anything that would make them feel important and involved. Persistence is the key—keep stating your objectives and asking questions until you form the group that will support you in this process.

．
．

In the end, create a budget that is a forward look at an exciting future. Then you will be in the psychological state for making it happen.

CHAPTER *nineteen*

How Do You Spell Relief?

:19 According to the old Rolaids™ commercial, when it came to indigestion, their name said it all. When it comes to settling our stomachs about money, most people would spell relief I - N - C - O - M - E. So if more dollars are the cure, we need to get creative for sure!

What ways have you thought of to increase your income? Are you limiting yourself based on your education, skills or the job market? Or have you found creative ways to access the abundance of wealth that exists?

Compensation comes in many forms. Let the curiosity you learned earlier lead you to inventive ways to accomplish what's in your financial plan.

Take A Minute:

We'll start by looking at some fairly traditional ways to increase your income, then we'll expand to the less conventional possibilities.

- ### Get a raise for your current position:

Go to the person who approves raises and ask them what it would take for you to get one. Ask about the raise you could expect, based on specific performance activity during a specific period of time. Let the person know your level of commitment to achieving those goals.

- **Get a promotion to a new position:**

Again, go to your supervisor and ask for details on how to promote to a higher-paying position.

- **Lower tax withholding:**

The more exemptions you claim, the bigger your paycheck, but you might end up owing at tax time. The best idea is to contact the Human Resources department, to ask if your withholdings are appropriate. Then ask them to analyze whether you can take more exemptions. Adjust accordingly, and review this position twice a year. If they aren't set up to do this, ask an accountant.

- **Get a second job:**

Getting a second job doesn't always mean working an additional forty, or even twenty, hours a week. Look at job possibilities, the wages they're paying and then calculate how many hours will equal the money you need.

- **Increase tax write-offs:**

Ask a new accountant to look at your old returns for new write-offs. Not all accountants are as adept at deductions as others, so you deserve to know if you're getting the most deductions you legally can.

- **Start your own business:**

You can get involved with an established business, like a network marketing company, or start a business of your own. Look for low overhead opportunities, like a babysitting service, simple lawn-care, or consulting.

- **Trade:**

Swap identical goods or services. This covers the income and expense category at the same time. For instance, if you're a massage therapist, trade massages with another therapist. For entrepreneurs, cross-promote through sharing databases. When I hold a class, I have business affiliates who send my class announcement to their list of contacts. It increases attendance and exposure, putting me in front of people I wouldn't know otherwise, and I do the same for them.

- **Barter:**

Swap different goods or services. So, if you can't pay for piano lessons for your child, think of something you can barter. Ask the piano teacher what services they need, and see if you can provide that service. Maybe you're an excellent woodworker, can baby-sit their children, or can offer to look after their pets while they're away.

- **Raise your fees:**

Find ways to add value to your business and raise your fees accordingly.

Make A Minute:

- Choose at least one possibility for increasing your income.

_____

_____

_____

_____

- Decide what actions to take to investigate or incorporate this possibility, schedule them, and record the results.

_____

_____

_____

_____

_____

.
.

Remember, affordability is a matter of desire. If there is something in your budget you say you can't afford, do you want it badly enough to get the money? If you do, find a way. If you don't, take it out of your budget. If it keeps showing up there's probably a reason, so take another look at how to creatively raise the money.

CHAPTER *twenty*

Step Away From The Remote!

:20 Now I'm going to challenge you to take another look at your expenses. We'll look at your everyday spending—including your cable bill—and examine how to restructure it to free up more money.

Let me first acknowledge the difficulty you might face in letting go of creature comforts you've come to depend on. I promise you'll find freedom in removing things that were an empty means to fulfillment. It may also be a good time to remind yourself of the free alternatives for meeting your needs, which you developed in Chapter 11.

Here are ten ways to reduce or eliminate some of your expenses:

- **Home phone:**

No one calls it anymore; you can use a cell phone for everything. At the very least, do away with all the extra phone service features, and buy an inexpensive message machine to replace voice mail.

- **Cell phone:**

If you must have a home phone, consider reducing your cell plan to the bare minimum. You can even have one that is strictly a 911 phone.

- **Groceries:**

There are two things that can dramatically impact what you spend at the grocery store, and this doesn't even include coupons!

  · Go once a week
  · Go with a list

More money is spent on emergency trips to the grocery store than you can imagine. It takes very little time to plan ahead, so decide what you'll spend and when you'll go.

- **Eating out:**

This used to be a special way to spend time, not just something to replace having to cook. Decide to make eating out an occasional special treat.

- **Cash:**

Only use cash for specific needs when you can't use checks or debit cards. Stop going to the ATM out of habit. There are very few things that can't be paid by debit card, which allows you to track your money more easily than using cash receipts.

- **Entertainment:**

This is another category of unconscious spending. As with the eating out section, plan your entertainment to be a special occasion, not just a diversion from life's aggravations.

- **Gifts:**

Categorize the gifts in your life; who gets them, when and why. Put limits on your spending, but remove limits on your sentiment. In other words, smaller gifts, bigger expressions of love, friendship or appreciation.

- **Cable/Satellite:**

Only you can determine how dependent you are on the television for entertainment. Review your cable bill for opportunities to save, and look for other ways to entertain yourself like games or reading.

- **Electricity/Gas:**

Get programmable thermostats and learn to use them. You can override them if you need to, but having them programmed for efficient usage can cut your bill significantly.

- **Clothing:**

Buy clothes at the end of the season and plan before you shop. Complete an inventory of your closet for exactly what you need and know when the annual or semi-annual sales occur.

Take A Minute:

- Look at each of your expenses on the budget you've started. Write down one way you can reduce or eliminate each expense, and by how much.
- Add it up.

Ways to reduce or eliminate expenses:

1. _____

2. _____

3. _____

4. _____

5. _____

6. _____

7. _____

8. _____

9. _____

10. _____

Total Savings:_____

What could that extra money do for you? It might pay for the vacation you've yearned for, or for a systematic retirement contribution. Don't look at it in terms of what's going away—look at the financial freedom those choices bring you, and focus on the excitement that comes with that.

Take Another Minute:

Review your mortgage, car payments, student loans or credit cards. Call your lenders to negotiate a better rate.

Do the same with other service bills—are better rates available? Ask your current company if they will meet or beat their competitors.

Make A Minute:

Choose which of your expenses to adjust, then choose where to apply the savings.

_____

_____

_____

_____

_____

:

One of the most effective financial choices you can make is to take better care of your possessions. Millions of dollars are spent each year to replace things that are lost, broken or spoiled. By paying attention to what you have, staying organized and caring for those things, you could easily save yourself a few hundred dollars a year.

CHAPTER *twenty-one*

Acting "As If"

:21 In the hit television show, *The Apprentice*, people line up by the thousands for a shot at working for Donald Trump. Confidence gets them on the show; confidence plus skill keeps them there. Confidence, plus skill, plus a little luck determines the ultimate winner.

Their confidence comes from behaving as if they've already won. Even when they don't walk away with the ultimate prize, many have capitalized on that confidence to get other professional positions or used it to make a great living speaking about their experiences. Without the ability to appear worthy of the role in the first place, where do you think they'd be?

You've created a powerful vision for your future, backed it up with strong declarations of intent, and created a financial map for where you want to go. Let's combine that with the process of physically acting as if you've arrived at your financial destination, to further ensure your success.

•
•

Acting "as if" is about learning to carry yourself with poise into financial situations by modeling examples of financial success: literally learning how to hold your head up in pursuit of your dreams. It doesn't mean acting like you suddenly have all the answers. It means projecting the self-assurance that you either know the answers or know you can get them.

If you've made some mistakes with money, you may be holding yourself back in the name of humility. If you're still walking around with your head bowed, that's not humility; it's humiliation. And there's a big difference, one you want to understand if you're going to take your rightful place in the financial world. Humiliation says, "I've made too many mistakes—I'll hold my head up when I've fixed everything." Humility says, "Where I've been is not who I am, and I am proudly creating a new financial future." Picture the physical difference in the person making those statements!

And, acting as if you've arrived at your goal creates an energy that propels you forward. It also produces a strong dynamic on which to build financial partnerships: instead of looking like you're completely dependent on someone for answers, you'll look like one who is ready for financial collaboration.

And finally, acting "as if" keeps you strong in the face of other people's doubt about your financial transformation. People are used to hearing how you were with money, not how you are now. So it's easy to revert to old patterns. You know how it is when you gather as a family for a holiday and everyone assumes their old roles, as if they were children again? The same can happen when you're on the move with your money but others aren't. People can try to hold you back without even knowing it. By literally standing firm in your financial resolve, you will teach them how to treat you, and be a great model for someone else's journey.

Take A Minute:

- Identify three people in your life who set an example of financial success to which you aspire.

1. _____

2. _____

3. _____

- Ask each of them for two beliefs or actions that make them financially successful.

1. _____

2. _____

3. _____

4. _____

5. _____

6. _____

- Choose at least one of those actions from each person to model in your life.

1. _____

2. _____

3. _____

- Practice these for at least two weeks.
- Record the results.

_____

_____

_____

_____

_____

Make A Minute:

More and more, you'll partner with financial professionals to reach your goals. When meeting with accountants, lawyers or financial planners, behave like you're ready for a financial partner, not a parent.

- Identify a financial scenario that intimidates you.

_____

_____

_____

- What must happen for you to feel financially confident?

_____

_____

_____

- Imagine those elements are in place. How does the "future you" walk in to the situation? What does your face look like? How do you dress? Walk? Stand? Sit? Which elements of success from your financial role models apply here?

_____

_____

_____

_____

_____

Make Another Minute:

- Act out your intimidating scenario.

Example:

Meet with a financial planner.

- Put yourself in "future mode" before calling for an appointment. Remind yourself of your financial confidence. Practice what you'll say before you get on the phone.
- Record the results.

_____

_____

_____

_____

_____

- On the day of the appointment, just before walking in to the office, put yourself in a confident state: stand, walk, dress and speak with total financial confidence.
- Record the results.

_____

_____

_____

_____

_____

．
．

A major factor in my financial recovery was my willingness to act as if I had moved on from my past, even when it didn't feel like I had. Fortunately, I had the support of great mentors who willingly shared their success strategies, and with their help I was able to make my way back to financial sanity. It's a joy to now pass those tips on to others.

You're worth whatever measures of financial success you want, so find your financial role models, copy their behavior until you develop your own, and pay it forward wherever you can!

CHAPTER twenty-two

K.I.S.S.
(Keep It Simple, Sweetie!)

22 There is no more pervasive financial question than "Where should I invest?" I will not be telling you the inner workings of every investment available—Suze Orman does that better than I. Instead I will give you a basic list of what to know about your goals before you ask a financial professional how to meet them.

I'll keep it simple. Matching your goals to the right financial vehicles isn't complicated as long as you're clear on where you want to go, when you want to get there, and how many ups and downs you can stand on the way. These—not what someone else thinks you should do—should dictate where you invest.

So, before we talk in the next chapter about choosing a financial professional, we'll determine your financial goals, your time frame for achieving them, and the amount of risk acceptable to you. Then when you meet with a financial planner, you'll be prepared to ask the right questions about investment and product options, the pro's and con's of each and be able to pick the options that make the most sense.

:

Let's clear something up before we go any further. There is a difference between investments and the financial product they are wrapped in. Investments include cash, stocks, bonds, mutual funds, real estate and commodities.

Financial products—like money markets, insurance, IRA's, 401(k)'s and trusts—provide benefits for those investments. So, cash is an investment, a money-market account is the wrapper that provides a small return and easy access to the money. Stocks are an investment, the IRA is the product that wraps them in tax protection.

There are risks and returns exclusive to both investments and products. Ask your financial professional to detail those so you can make investment *and* product choices that match your goals.

Take A Minute:

This exercise goes hand-in-hand with the previous budgeting exercises. At that time, you identified bigger needs than your daily expenses, perhaps college savings or a retirement goal. You determined the general costs and an idea of how you'll save for them. Now you'll develop more specific information that determines the investment or savings plan for these goals.

- The first step is to decide what your investment goals are. List five of them.

1. _____

2. _____

3. _____

4. _____

5. _____

Make A Minute:

Next, decide what your time frame is for achieving them. It can be a set point in the future, or involve a range of dates, such as five to ten years.

1. _____   Time Frame: _____

2. _____   Time Frame: _____

3. _____   Time Frame: _____

4. _____   Time Frame: _____

5. _____   Time Frame: _____

Make Another Minute:

Now ask yourself how much risk you can take on these investments. Risk comes in many forms, but the two most likely are return on the money invested—or how much loss of principle you can risk—and the ability to access your investments with little or no penalty.

In the case of return on the investment, if we're working with the example of saving for college, would growing the investment from $10,000 to $30,000 be great, but ending up at $20,000 be okay? If so, that means you can risk a greater fluctuation in your returns.

In terms of accessing funds without penalty, you need to know exactly what your time frames are so you can pick an investment that matches. You don't want to get to your time goal only to find there's a high surrender charge for accessing the investment. At the same time, a small penalty may be worth the rate of return you'll get. You don't have to know which penalties are specific to which investments yet, just what your general tolerance is for them.

What risks can you tolerate with each goal?

Goal	Risk
1. _____	_____
2. _____	_____
3. _____	_____
4. _____	_____
5. _____	_____

．
．

I know this seems like a highly simplistic way to approach investing, but I can promise you that preparing these details before you meet with a financial planner puts you way ahead of the game. You're doing your part to create a financial partnership you can feel great about by doing your homework ahead of meeting with them: it says you're serious about your financial intentions when you're able to meet them half-way with the details of what really matters to you.

CHAPTER twenty-three

Chuck, Merrill Or Raymond

:23 When it's time to invest, to whom will you go? To a friend, or a friend of a friend? Broker or Certified Financial Planner? Paid hourly or on commission? Not knowing how to answer these questions often keeps people from doing anything at all.

Here's a revelation: no matter what kind of planner you work with, there are pro's and con's to every choice. There is no perfect answer.

With that epiphany out of the way, I'll give you what I consider to be some absolutes in choosing a financial professional. Then we'll discuss what to do with them, and how to know when it's time to find a new advisor.

Absolutely:

- Interview at least three advisors: commission-only, fee only and someone who is paid both ways. Share the same financial goal with each of them, then compare how each would manage it from a product *and* cost standpoint. Look for whether they're really helping you plan or just selling a product.
- Get all your questions answered before you choose your planner. This includes how each product works, the pro's and con's, and how they apply to your scenario. Don't worry about what

you don't know; address what you need to know. You will hear things you don't understand but don't give your power away by saying "I don't know what you're talking about." Instead, stay curious, using empowering questions or statements to get your answers.

Examples:
- "I need you to go back and explain specifically how this product applies to my situation."
- "Say more about that."
- "What are the worst-case scenarios and the best-case scenarios with this product?"

Keep asking questions until you're satisfied that you understand what they're presenting.

Find someone who has at least five years experience, or who is supported in their office by someone who does. If you choose to work with someone very new, make it clear that you expect their superior's involvement.

•
•

Once you've chosen someone, you'll need to agree on certain things, such as how to invest your money and the frequency of your communication.

You have the information you developed in the previous chapter about your goals and their time horizons. You also decided what amount of risk you could tolerate on your returns and what liquidity of assets you need. In addition to working with your advisor on traditional investment choices, I'd ask you to look at choosing investments from an additional angle, one that can help you feel an even deeper interest in where you put your money.

There's a great life-coaching question that asks, "What would you do if you knew you couldn't fail?" My financial version is, "Where would you invest if you knew you couldn't fail, and why?"

If you knew you couldn't fail, from what standpoint would you choose your investments? Maybe you would buy stocks of companies whose products you enjoy, or of companies that support your strong environmental stance. Maybe bonds would appeal to you because of the community infrastructure they support. From this new perspective, you might invest in real estate for the sake of what you could do to improve a neighborhood.

Consider adding this "why else" thinking to your investment strategy. If it's only about the money, the slightest move that's not on the upswing can be stressful. Balance your decisions about rate of return with other ways that it pays for you to be in the investment—get more connected to it. Not attached, but connected. More connected means more aware, and more aware means more able to spot trends that will affect your decisions in the long run.

Remember, don't choose any investment that you don't completely understand.

⋮

Being more connected to your investments includes understanding the statements that you'll periodically receive. It's up to you to know how to read them and to keep track of your progress between visits with your planner. During your early meetings, simply ask them to explain how to read the statements you'll receive.

As far as knowing how often to review the returns on your investment, it depends on your time frame. If it's a retirement account, and the time horizon is more than fifteen years, then semi-annual or annual reviews should be sufficient. If it's a shorter-term investment, consider asking for quarterly reviews. In all cases, you should expect to meet with your advisor as often as you need to feel well informed.

Keep the bond with your advisor strong by staying involved. A productive relationship takes time and attention. Make sure you're doing your part and you'll be in a great position to see that they are also.

Take A Minute:

Decide—do you have the relationship with a financial advisor that you want?

Make A Minute:

Commit to interviewing new planners or re-interviewing the one you have, to ensure you're with the right one.

•
•

There may come a time when you want a new advisor. First determine if you've held up your end of the deal by communicating life changes that affect your investments and participated in regular reviews. If you've done your part, but they're not doing theirs, you should express this directly.

There may be penalties for moving your investments, so work to correct the problem first, either by getting their commitment to change or by asking for another advisor within the same firm. If you know you want to move your money, understand the penalties; if you've decided the move is worth that, then do it. You don't owe anyone an apology for leaving, but an explanation might go a long way toward helping the advisor improve for future clients.

•
•

When working with any professionals regarding your finances, ask everything you need to know to determine if it's the right partnership. It's your money, and you deserve professional relationships that support you and your goals.

CHAPTER twenty-four

You, CEO

:24 The only things for certain, they say, are death and taxes. The other thing for sure is that if you don't have a system for managing your money, you'll never get what you say you want. So let's give you an easy method of accountability, one that keeps up-to-date financial information at your fingertips.

Before I go further, you should know I'll be recommending computer and Internet technology in these systems. There are some who'd rather have their fingernails pulled out than pay bills online. Some of you don't think you can learn it and some of you think it isn't safe.

You can learn it. The learning curve might be steep, but I promise that once you get the process, it will never be that hard again. That being said, I won't claim your success is conditional upon tracking things electronically.

And it's no more dangerous to pay bills online than it is to give your credit card to a waiter. It's just as easy for them to disappear and copy the information as it is for someone to hack into it online. But again, I won't insist on it.

I will insist that you do something. You can't do all this wonderful work of improving what comes into your mind and out of your mouth about money, and not change how you manage it. So, whether you do it by computer program or with a good, old-fashioned ledger, the point is that you do it—consistently and well.

Great businesses have strong systems. You run the system, and the system runs the business. This keeps you working on the bigger picture for your business, not on the day-to-day minutiæ all the time.

The same is true for your financial life. By creating systems for tracking your progress and running them on a regular basis, you get more time to enjoy your life. Paper doesn't pile up waiting to be tended to. You don't waste time wondering if you have the financial means for something. You get a clear sense of where you are and what to do to improve. Then you can make it happen, instead of wondering or worrying about how to do it.

Some of you have great money management systems in your life already. There are always ways to improve, so use this information to enhance what's working.

I'll share my system, including my daily, weekly, monthly, semi-annual and annual action items. It includes sorting the mail, balancing your checkbook and incorporating the above-mentioned technology to assist you in streamlining these processes.

Daily:

I open bills immediately. I actually use a very nice letter opener to do this, because I believe in creating a great physical environment for my money. I used to rip through the bills, now I carefully open them.

I sit down at the computer and enter the new bill amounts into my Microsoft® Money™ program, which I use for all my accounts. For the bills I will pay online, I schedule them to be paid at least two days before the due date. For those that need to be mailed, I schedule to pay them at least seven days in advance of the due date. I make time each day to open, record and schedule the bills.

I then file the paper version in a folder labeled, "Bills to be paid."

Take A Minute:
What are the daily actions to take with your money?

_____

_____

_____

Weekly:
Once a week I make deposits that haven't already been made electronically and sit down to pay bills. I usually do this on Tuesday because that's when the banks have cleared information they received over the weekend. My Money™ program alerts me to which are due to be paid because of the way I scheduled them when I originally entered them.

Again, in the interest of feeling good while I work, I do two things: I play music to raise my energy, and I take every opportunity to say "thank you" as I pay them, whether on the actual memo section of the check, or aloud as I click the submit button to pay them online.

I start by downloading my bank information into my Money™ program to update that information first; then I pay the bills that are due. I pay all bills online, as they come due or by Electronic Funds Transfer. Those that require a check get paid by snail mail. When I'm done paying the bills, I file what needs to be kept and shred what doesn't. For a list of statements that you need to keep, consult your accountant.

Take Another Minute:
What are the weekly actions to take with your money?

_____

_____

_____

Monthly:

Once a month, I review my budget to see what spending has been within the guidelines and what hasn't. Based on that information I strategize the changes in spending or saving to make for the next month.

This is a good time to balance your checkbook if you're doing all this manually. Coordinate monthly financial activities with the receipt of your bank statement.

I also receive investment statements every month, so I review them, calculate the returns and decide if anything further needs to be done—like talking to my advisor (who happens to be my husband!).

Take Another Minute:

What are the monthly actions to take with your money?

_____

_____

_____

Quarterly:

Quarterly, I do an income and expense projection. This is the easiest of all: I write what still needs to be accomplished financially, the associated costs, and then my projected income. Based on that information, I'll need to cover a shortfall, or be enjoying an excess. If I'm short on funds, I think of how I can be creative in making it up. My belief is that I can create the means to meet my needs, if my needs are important enough. If I'm enjoying a surplus, I decide where to apply it.

Take Another Minute:

What are the quarterly actions to take with your money?

_____

_____

_____

Semi-Annually:

Semi-annually, I receive other investment reports, which I review as before. This is also when I review my profit for the year, (which means retained earnings that were directed to savings or investments), and plan additional strategies for meeting my annual goals.

Take Another Minute:

What are the semi-annual actions to take with your money?

_____

_____

_____

Annually:

Annually, I not only do a recap of where I've been; I also have a summit with my husband to decide our goals for the next year.

I gather the banking, investment, credit card and charitable contribution information to send to my accountant, shred anything that I don't need to keep, and start files for the new year.

Take Another Minute:

What are the annual actions to take with your money?

_____

_____

_____

This system is really simple, but I won't pretend it was completely easy to do in the beginning. Now that I've learned how to do it, nothing takes more than an hour to complete. I have so much more time now for the things I enjoy that it was worth the time and initial frustration of learning to do it. And by treating my money like a business, it has paid me like one.

．
．
．

There are people who love the computer and learn every nuance of a program like Money™ or Quicken™. I can't honestly say I'm one of them. I have learned what I need to make my money work, and I have complete confidence in my ability to ask for help when needed. This is my wish for you: become so sure of your ability to learn new things and ask for help, that nothing financial seems insurmountable.

Rolling Around Naked In A Pile Of Money

"Rolling around naked in a pile of money": that's what someone at one of my seminars thought I meant by financial intimacy. By now you know that financial intimacy is the essential knowledge of what money means to you; an awareness so connected to your true nature that success with attracting and managing money becomes inevitable.

This understanding has come to you or been strengthened by your remarkable commitment to applying these exercises to your life; they will continue to support your financial success for as long as you stay connected to them.

So, to anchor this knowledge one last time, let's review the subjects you have become intimately familiar with as a result of this work:

Writing a new money story · *Replacing financial fear with faith* · Directing your financial focus · *Cultivating gratitude* · Creating self-worth greater than net-worth · *Getting curious* · Financial attraction · *Empowering language* · Gauging desire · *Meeting your needs* · Choosing new meanings · *Weighing ideas* · How to say "No" · *How to say "Thank You"* · Plugging into your energy · *Defining your life* · Aligning your partners · *Increasing income* · Decreasing expenses · *Modeling success* · Professional partnership · *Directing your investments* · **The business of your financial life!**

Never forget what it means to be financially free. This freedom isn't just about money. It's the freedom to plan the future and to enjoy the present. It's the freedom to personally expand and to serve others. It's the freedom to know financial answers or where to get them. All of this is possible, no matter what your financial status, if you're diligent about changing your thoughts, words and actions regarding money.

$$\vdots$$

Remember the movie *City Slickers?* Curly, the crusty, old, ranch hand, mysteriously alludes to the one thing Billy Crystal needs to know that will change him forever, but Curly dies before revealing the secret.

There's no single thing to know about money, but there is one thing you can do, every day, to change your financial life. Are you ready?

That's it—that's the secret. There is one thing you can do differently every day that will change your financial story. All you need to do is seize the opportunity.

Maybe the one thing is choosing a new way to think. Maybe it's organizing your tax records for the year. Maybe it's simply opening a portion of a stack of bills. Take a minute to do at least one thing, every day, for your finances and your results will change for the better, forever.

Take A Minute:

Ask yourself, "What's the one thing I can do today to change my financial life?"

_____

_____

_____

_____

Make A Minute:

Commit to one financial action every day for the next thirty and record what changes as a result.

_____

_____

_____

_____

_____

_____

_____

_____

_____

_____

∴

Here are my final thoughts on the subject:

I believe that we have the freedom in a spiritual sense to discover all of the beauty the world has to offer, that we all deserve to experience whatever goodness God, Spirit or the Universe has made. I believe we also have a spiritual responsibility for being financially fit enough to experience it. What experiences are waiting for you in the world?

And each of you has amazing talents that the world can't experience when your money trouble is standing in the way. Your spiritual responsibility extends to how you can serve others with your talents, so what part of *you* is the world waiting to experience?

Everything you want out of life is available if you help enough people get what they want too. My last challenge to you, therefore, is to gather in groups, as often as you can, to break the silence around money and to support each other in reaching your goals. We can change how people relate to money and make it easier for everyone to find success by refusing to stay quiet on the subject.

And lastly, my life is different—better—because of you, because of your willingness to make a move with your money and grow. By sharing your hope for a better life, you help keep mine alive. I am more grateful than you know, and as I take a minute each day to express my gratitude for you, I hope you, too, will make a minute to express your gratitude for whatever keeps you moving on the path to your financial dreams!

Appendix

Appendix A: Personal Budget

INCOME	JAN	FEB	MAR	APR	MAY	JUN	JUL	AUG	SEP	OCT	NOV	DEC
Paycheck												
Paycheck												
Commissions												
Investment Inc.												
Other Income												
Other Income												
Total Income:												
EXPENSES												
Auto Gas/Service												
Auto Payments												
Auto Insurance												
Bank Charges												
Charity												
Childcare												
Clothing												
Dining Out												
Education												
Entertainment												
Gifts												
Groceries												
HOA												

Income	JAN	FEB	MAR	APR	MAY	JUN	JUL	AUG	SEP	OCT	NOV	DEC
Home Maintenance												
Household Items												
Insurance: Home												
Insurance: Health												
Insurance: Other												
Insurance: Other												
Medical Expense												
Mortgage Payment												
Miscellaneous												
Taxes												
Telephone												
Utilities												
Utilities												
Utilities												
Other												
Other												
Other												
Total Expenses												
Income minus Expenses												

SAVE...and WALK TALL

Your savings, believe it or not, affect the way you stand, the way you walk, the tone of your voice...in short, your physical well-being and self-confidence. A man without savings is always running. He must. He must take the first job offered, or nearly so. He sits nervously on life's chairs because any small emergency throws him into the hands of others.

Without savings, a man must be grateful. Gratitude is a fine thing in its place. But a constant state of gratitude is a horrible place in which to live. A man with savings can **WALK TALL**. He may appraise opportunities in a relaxed way, have time for judicious estimates and not be rushed by economic necessity.

A man with savings can afford to resign from his job, if his principles so dictate. And, for this reason, he'll never need to do so. A man who can afford to quit is much more useful to his company, and therefore more promotable. He can afford to give his company the benefit of his most candid judgment.

A man always concerned about necessities, such as food and rent, can't afford to think in long-range career terms.

A man with savings can afford the wonderful privilege of being generous in family or neighborhood emergencies. He can take a level stare from the eyes of any man...friend, stranger, or enemy.

It shapes his personality and his character.

The ability to save has nothing to do with the size of income. Many high-income people, who spend it all, are on a treadmill, darting through life like minnows.

The Dean of American Brokers, J.P. Morgan, once advised a young broker: "Take waste out of your spending and you'll drive the haste out of your life."

If you don't need money for college, a home or retirement, then save for self-confidence. The state of your savings does have a lot to do with how **TALL YOU WALK**.

—Author Unknown

Resources

One of the messages I got early in my financial recovery is that my success would be shaped by what I read and who I hung out with. So, here is a partial list of what I've read and who I've hung out with that I hope will be of help to you on your journey to financial freedom.

Books:

Nice Girls Don't Get Rich—75 Avoidable Mistakes Women Make With Money, Lois P. Frankel, pub. 2005, Warner Books

Think And Grow Rich, Napoleon Hill, pub. 1984, Aventine Press

Smart Women Finish Rich, David Bach, pub. 2002, Broadway Books

The Energy of Money, Maria Nemeth, pub. 2000, Random House

Money Drunk, Money Sober, Mark Bryan & Julia Cameron, pub. 1999, Random House

You Don't Have To Be Rich, Jean Chatzky, pub. 2003, Portfolio

The Courage To Be Rich, Suze Orman, pub. 2001, Riverhead Trade

The Seven Spiritual Laws Of Success, Deepak Chopra, pub. 1995, New World Library/Amber-Allen Publishing

Secrets of Six-Figure Women, Barbara Stanny, pub. 2004, Collins

The Millionaire Next Door, Thomas J. Stanley, pub. 1996, Simon & Schuster

The Richest Man in Babylon, George S. Clason, pub. 1989, Dutton Adult

I also thoroughly enjoy the "Love & Money" column by Jeff Opdyke in *The Wall Street Journal* each week.

Web Sites:

www.bankrate.com—Filled with comparison rates for mortgages, savings, small business, credit cards and more. Wonderful goal calculators for every category.

www.google.com—Any subject, any time, faster than a speeding bullet.

www.msnmoney.com—A great site for easy-to-understand financial tips.

www.morningstar.com—A free membership site, with great Q&A on personal finance.

www.about.com—Everything you ever wanted to know about, well, everything. A great place to go to research particular topics.

www.jeanchatzky.com—A wonderful site, full of helpful money tips.

People/Programs:

Debtors Anonymous—Consider this twelve-step approach to recovery from problems with overspending and debt.
www.debtorsanonymous.org

Anthony Robbins—Unleash The Power Within—A weekend seminar to help you break through the barriers in your mind to success.
www.anthonyrobbins.com

Women On Fire, Vision Day—Two events offered by the coaches of GroupMV, Debbie Phillips and Rob Berkley, the first is a gathering of women from across the country, who come together to support what each is "on fire" about in their life. The second, *Vision Day*, is a day devoted to you and your vision, in the wonderful environments of Martha's Vineyard, or Naples, Florida.
www.groupmv.com/www.visionday.com

eWomenNetwork—A great women's networking organization, with close to one hundred chapters worldwide. Great support, networking and speakers.
www.ewomennetwork.com

Volunteers of America—Want to give back to the community, but not sure where to start? VOA is a national, non-profit, spiritually-based organization that provides local human service programs of every kind.
www.voa.org

•
•

I welcome any information about books, sites, people and programs that you'd like to see added to future editions and put on our web site. Please send information of this kind to resources@afinancialminute.com.

Index

A

abundance, 52

accomplishments, taking stock
 of, 53–55, 94–95

advisors, financial, 127–130

affirmations, 28

"as if," 117–122

assertiveness, need for 85–86

attitude,
 assessing, 11–13, 19–21
 improving, 43–48

attraction theory, 49–52

attributes, personal, 59–64

B

bartering, 111

beliefs, 20–21

bills

routines for, 132–136

software for paying, 132, 133,
 136

borrowing, faith, 28

budget
 defining, 77–78
 for fulfillment, 100–104
 form for, 143–144
 getting support for, 105–108,
 140
 materials for, 106
 minute for, 78

C

children, involving in budget,
 107–100

compliments, accepting, 89–92
 minute for, 91

consumerism, 33, 37–41

    and self–worth, 38–39

curiosity, 43–46

E

exemptions, tax, 110

expenses, reducing, 113–116

F

faith, defined, 23

family, 18, 21, 107–108

fears, about money, 25–27

financial planner

    meeting with, 120–121

    selecting, 127–130

focus, 29, 32

    minute for, 30–32

G

gift-buying, 85–87

goals, 99–104

    affording, 65–70

    investment, 124–125

    reasonable, 71–72

gratitude, 34–36

    minute for, 34

I

income, increasing, 109–112

intimacy, financial, 137

investing goals, 124–126

L

language

    budget and, 77–78

    of sabotage, 62

    of self, 59–61

limitations, defining by finances, 65–70

mantra, for money, 31–32

minute

    for accepting compliments, 91

    for attracting money, 50–52

    for banishing negativity, 44–48

    for beliefs, 20–21, 30–32

    for budget, 78

    to celebrate progress, 53–55

    for confidence, 91

    for defining needs, 73

    for determining an outcome, 102–104

    for expectations of money, 51–52

    on faith, 24

    for focus, 30–32

    for gratitude, 34–36

    for increasing income, 111

    initial assessment, 11–13

    for making steady improvement, 139

    "money story," 19–20

    for reducing expenses, 115–116

for role models, 119–120

perceptions about money, 83–84

M

mission, personal, 61–62

money

    affirmations about, 28

    being assertive about, 85–86

    beliefs about, 20–21

    expectations of, 49–52

    fears about, 25–27

    mantra, 31–32

    perceptions about, 11–13, 19–20, 81–84

    Money Mantra, 31–32

"money story," 17–21

N

needs

    charting, 74, 75, 76

    defining, 71–76

    minute for, 73

negativity, banishing, 43–48

    minute for, 44–48

O

office, financial traps of, 85–86

P

payoff, 20

perceptions, 81–84

personal mission, defining, 61–62

personal power statement

    defining, 60–63

preconceptions, 81–84

R

resources, 145–147

rewarding self, 55

risk, acceptable, 125–126

routine, for finances, 132–135

S

savings

    budget for, 107

    Save and Walk Tall, 145

self-worth

    assessing, 40, 41

    defining, 60–63

stuff, focusing on having, 37–41

systems, for bill paying, 132–135

T

taxes, finding write-offs, 110

V

visualization, 31, 32

W

wants

    determining outcome, 99–104

    minute for, 102–104

wants vs. needs

    determining, 71–76

    minute for, 73

Jenifer Madson

Jenifer Madson's professional experience spans fifteen years of coaching people in the key areas of relationships and money—first as the owner of a dating business, then as a financial services broker. She now teaches people how to get what they want by improving their relationship *with* money.

She has built multi-million dollar franchise territories for the dating industry, led award-winning branch offices for a national financial services firm and developed an international coaching clientele. She is a phenomenal example of what can happen from applying the principles of her work—she has absolutely "walked her talk." Her great mission is to teach people to attract and manage money for the sake of what they love—to truly be financially free!

Clients include: **Aegon International** · **Price Waterhouse Coopers** · **U.S. Government** · **American Health Radiology Administrators** · **NYSE** · **Ladies' Workout Express** · **Sales Pros International** · **eWomenNetwork** · **Micro Business Development** · **WIRE: Women In Real Estate** · **LifeMoxie**

Jenifer can be reached by phone, e-mail or through the web, and welcomes your comments and suggestions:

303-664-1947
jenifer@afinancialminute.com
www.afinancialminute.com

Please visit our web site, **www.afinancialminute.com**, to sign up for the weekly e-column, "A Financial Minute w/Jenifer," **free** tips on the emotional *and* practical techniques for financial success.

Don't forget to visit the coaching and programs page of our web site for information on joining the **Financial Freedom Forum**, a group coaching program applying the principles of this book, for people ready to break through their financial limitations and truly be financially free!

And check the calendar on the web site to find when Jenifer will be visiting a city near you!

Order Form

Give the gift of *A Financial Minute* to
your friends, family and colleagues.

Several ways to order:
- · Your local bookstore
- · On the web, at **www.afinancialminute.com**
- · Fax this form to **303-484-4937**
- · E-mail: **orders@afinancialminute.com**
- · Mail this form with check or money order payable to:
  Clear Vision Press
  2382 Norfolk St.
  Erie, CO 80516

Item	Unit Cost	Qty.	Subtotal
A Financial Minute			
Applicable State Sales Tax			
Shipping & Handling			$5.00
		Total:	$

Credit Card: ☐ Visa ☐ MasterCard ☐ Discover ☐ Amex

Card #: _____ Exp. Date: _____

Signature: _____

Name on card: _____

Address: _____

City, State, Zip: _____

Ship to:

Name: _____

Address: _____

City, State, Zip: _____

Printed in the United States
53026LVS00002B/241-261